Random Thoughts From A Diseased Mind (Not For Dummies)

John L.R. Linde

Bloomington, IN  Milton Keynes, UK

authorHOUSE

AuthorHouse™
1663 Liberty Drive, Suite 200
Bloomington, IN 47403
www.authorhouse.com
Phone: 1-800-839-8640

AuthorHouse™ UK Ltd.
500 Avebury Boulevard
Central Milton Keynes, MK9 2BE
www.authorhouse.co.uk
Phone: 08001974150

First published by AuthorHouse 4/8/2006

ISBN: 1-4259-1978-2 (sc)

Cover photo by Rosita Thomas.

Printed in the United States of America
Bloomington, Indiana

This book is printed on acid-free paper.

This book is dedicated to....no...strike that.... shoved in the faces of all those who never thought I'd be worth a damn. You are the people who made me the sick fucker I am today....thanks bunches, assholes.

Actually, this book IS dedicated to all those who believed in me, helped me out through the hard times, and mean the most to me in the world! They are(in no particular order): My grandmother Margaret(who raised me to be a relatively decent person), the love of my life Rose(without whose love and support, this book would never have happened), and my (future) stepchildren Krystal and Karl. Last, but not least, my two best male friends, Dennis and Mike. I love you all, and you are the reason I'm still alive. Thanks for putting up with me. Sharon, you can kiss my ass. You know who you are, and why.

Acknowledgements: Thanks go out to George Carlin(my favorite comedian), who opened my eyes to just how fucked up the world is. You inspired me to humour, and showed me that the world is well worth laughing at. If you don't find humour in everyday life, it's liable to kill you. Thanks also go out to Steven Brust(my favorite writer), for not only giving me literature worth reading, but for helping me to follow my dream of being a published writer. Thank you for answering every e-mail I've sent you. One last group to be thanked...the American People. You just keep doing stupid shit that keeps me entertained, and with no shortage of material.

Oh man, where do I begin...let's start with the basics, I am a 35 year old American Male. One pure-bred Honkey. Generation-X to the maX. Notice, I didn't say PROUD American. Even before that Sept. 11 shit, I've been the most apathetic motherfucker this side of George Carlin. I see the flags waving, and I'm not impressed. Every dick in America is now a card carrying, flag waving, patriot. My ass. Actually, most of that shit had passed by mid January. Americans are secure again. No more planes ramming into buildings, no more retards trying to set their sneakers on fire, and the only Anthrax in sight is the rock band. America is getting back to normal. It's over people, back to the same old hum-drum killing each other in the streets over petty shit. Time to start driving like idiots again, cuz if we don't...THEY HAVE WON! America is going back to the pre-Sept. 11 norm. Like this is a GOOD THING!

This country is full of idiots, and to find proof, all anyone needs to do is watch the evening news. Like that Andrea Yates thing, that goofy bitch drowns her five fucking kids. Her husband...this guy should run as Gary Condit's VP running mate! He defends her, saying that she is a warm loving person. Yep. Every great mom, who is a warm loving person, at least the ones that I have met, have all drowned their kids! I say we lock him up too!

Can anyone remember the name of that other ditzy slut who locked her kids in the car and shoved it into the lake?

Did anyone happen to catch that Celebrity Boxing show? It was rather stupid, and I tell you this, I'm glad as shit MY name wasn't attached to that mess! Everyone involved, their careers, what little tidbit they had left...shot to shit. I did come off with some clever quips though, while Barry Williams was getting his ass handed to him by Danny Bonaduce. Every time Danny busted him in the face, I yelled "MARSHA MARSHA MARSHA!" I also came up with a wild T-Shirt idea... "Danny 3:16" on the front(for those non-WWF fans, that comes from the Austin 3:16 reference) with a picture of Bonaduce's face on the back, from when he was Partridge Family age. You know, it's a sad state of affairs when you realize that Vanilla Ice can fight better than Greg Brady. At least Ice put up a fight. I don't like him, never did, and probably never will, but at least he has a decent chin. The show was pathetic, but had its moments.

That's another thing that is seriously fucked up about this country, there are literally hundreds of channels available to the average American, and there is maybe 8 hours of decent programming on every week. Way too much garbage on TV. No wonder 'The Children' are fucked in the head, look at the crap they are exposed to! From infancy on up. It starts with Barney and the Tele-Tubbies, Sesame Street and Mr. Rogers, moves onto whatever cartoon the neighbors kid is watching, and ends up with them shooting up their school. I've compiled a rather short list of decent shit worth watching on TV. South Park, The Osborne's, Jeopardy, The Simpsons, King of the Hill, Weakest Link(the British version only, America even managed to fuck that concept up!), Futurama, and for those with HBO, OZ. Not much on TV worth watching these days. CNN can be entertaining once in a while, like when a disaster happens. I prefer the local stations for my news though, I get to find out what kind of idiots are living within driving distance.

Reality TV has got to GO! This shit got ancient before it first aired. I checked out "Survivor" once... apparently their definition of "Survival" is different from mine. I was rather hoping that if you couldn't survive, you died. Now THAT would be reality TV for me! Strand a bunch of fuckers on an island and make them REALLY survive that shit. Put a sign on the landing pad; "This ain't Gilligan's Island, all but one of you are going to die." Watch how many people sign up for that show! Get voted off, what the fuck kind of concept is that? And where do you go? You go back to the hotel and feel like a complete loser. Stick me on an island, and offer me a Million to get my own way home, and my ass will be back on the mainland within a month!

Here's a reality show we'll probably never see, stick 20 people on a boat 20 miles out in the ocean during a hurricane, blow a hole in the hull just below the waterline, and whoever can get to dry land and not require an amputation wins a million bucks.

How about a reality show about Road Rage? That could be funny! And on that note, bring back the demolition derby! Maybe combine the two!

A short list of people who need to be disemboweled with a salad fork: Britney Spears, Yoko Ono, Gilbert Gottfried, NSync, the Backstreet Boys, that asshole who hosts the American version of Weakest Link, all country singers who do cover versions of any top 40 hit, and anyone who uses a cell phone while driving!

Speaking of cell phones, to all of you out there who use them in your vehicle, in a store, walking down the street, wherever and whenever that doesn't include an emergency... understand something, you really aren't that important, you look stupid, and you are some of the most annoying fucks walking upright. There is no phone call in the universe that is that important. Why do you even leave home/office/etc... If you are expecting a really important call? I love to annoy you bastards. My dick gets hard when I see some self-important shitball yacking on a cell phone. I see that, and my 'cell phone radar' sends a signal right to my dick. Then a secondary signal gets sent out to my mouth. The next thing you know, the words "HONEY! COME BACK TO BED!" Or "I SAID GRAB THE K-Y! NOT THE

PHONE!" These statements can usually cut someone right off. Right in mid-word. I've seen it happen. Before I came up with those, I used to just run up and demand an autograph, all the while yelling "SOMEONE IMPORTANT!!! GIMME AN AUTOGRAPH!! I'M A HUGE FAN!!!" Just to embarrass them. Not only embarrass them, but to disrupt the call. Anything for a distraction.

Here's a funny little story, it's true, I swear it. Back in September, this was maybe a week or so after the attacks, me and my girlfriend were riding along, and saw these two kids(maybe early teens) standing on a street corner, painted up like the American flag. Only wearing a pair of shorts and shoes. I flipped them the bird as we rode past, cuz they were waving to everyone, and looking like a pair of "shouldabeenaborteds". The look of shock on their faces was absolutely priceless. Hey, dipshit, welcome to the REAL world. Anyway, about an hour or so later, we came back past the other way, and they were about a mile up the road. They spotted us, and I flipped them off again, they started jumping up and down, yelling "Fuck you!" And that kinda shit. They returned the finger, and the really funny part was, no one saw us flip them off, just them screaming "Fuck You!" and apparently flipping off everyone in sight while painted as the American Flag. I laughed so hard I almost pissed myself.

I mentioned my girlfriend, and even this soon into the book, you must be wondering what kind of sick minded bitch would hook up with me. I can only say four words in answer to that.........I'm bad, she's worse! Something else I should mention about her, some of the ideas in this book were suggested by her, and all the ones I came up with were run past her.

I also mentioned that I am Generation-X. Where the fuck did the rest of you go? Actually, I know. Most of you were posers to begin with. I'm beginning to think I am the sole survivor of that mentality. If I am, well, BFD. The rest of you want to evolve, go with the flow, grow up? Fine with me. More targets for my sharp tongue. Sell outs, each and every one of you. Just like that threesome of sissies, Metallica.

Speaking of those losers, did I miss something somewhere along the line? Did they or did they not admit to copying each others records and tapes? I read it somewhere, I think it was Rolling Stone, where Lars and Hetfield admitted it. And yet they bitched about Napster. Explain the difference to me, except for the fact that it was their shit being copied, and not someone else's. Oh, when they were doing it, it was fine and dandy. Actually, it was more than just them it was being done to, but still, who cares? It didn't cost them penny one. Every Napster user knows it, because most of us were either downloading shit we already had(and had paid for!) or stuff we weren't going to buy in the first place.

Why is it that most sequels suck? Cases in point; Aliens, Temple of Doom, The Toxic Avenger II, Batman Returns, Return to Blue Lagoon, and a whole bunch more. And why is it that prequels always suck harder? Maybe because you already know where the story is going?

Speaking of movies, there has been a whole lot of that re-doing, re-editing, directors cut, etc...kind of movies coming out lately. What the fuck is that shit about? This reminds me of that big stink that Ted Turner created with those colorized movies. Same shit. Who says history never repeats? Some of those movies actually DO turn out ok, if not really cool. Case in point, is the re-do's on the Star Wars movies. They were all FX shots, and stuff that would have been done when the movie was made had the technology been in place. Some of those movies really sucked the big wet fart. For an example, I present Planet of the Apes. This one, as opposed to the original, required all the fx in the world to carry it, shame it didn't work. Or not. I grant you, the original set whole new standards for make-up jobs, but the technology for any elaborate special effects simply didn't exist. So the original relied on a great story, and incredible make-up work to create a great movie. A true classic in every sense of the word. The remake, however, is a classic...example of how to really fuck up a great movie concept. Hell, even the Planet of the Apes TV show ranks in my top 20 great shows of all time, but the new movie isn't even worth watching for free.

And what the fuck is up with re-doing E.T.? And for a TV presentation nonetheless! The thing that really sticks in my craw(what the fuck IS a craw, anyway?) is the question of why did they remove an element of the original, specifically for the 20th anniversary airing? I'm talking about the scene that they took the guns out of the polices hands? Who's brilliant idea was this? Are we supposed to be sending kids the message that the police would not react with drawn weapons knowing an alien of unknown origin and what threat condition said creature may represent? If this is the message we are sending them, why should they think a drug dealer on the street corner would be considered more of a threat than an unknown alien hence think the police would be even more apprehensive about drawing their weapons.

You know, it's probably a good thing I'm not a parent. I'm the type who would display the "My kid beat the shit out of your honor student" bumper sticker. And mean it! My kid would probably also kick the crap out of your kid in Trivial Pursuit, Jeopardy, and pretty much any other knowledge related game/game show.

Many of you may feel like I am a serious Anti-American Asshole. BFD. Fine, feel that way. I really could give a fuck less, but it isn't worth the effort. I'm not against the constitution, nor am I against the basic principles this country was allegedly founded upon. I've just seen enough to know that no one has ever adhered to the principles this country was founded upon. The government is a lying, self important, self righteous, preserve the power structure organization that takes it's own self interest above the personal freedoms, liberties, and pursuits of happiness of those it has sworn to protect and serve.

Getting back to the whole movie thing, I figured out why the guns were removed from the E.T. Movie. To "protect the children." If this isn't the biggest crock of shit. Every least little thing we can think of, gets banned, prohibited, outlawed, all that happy shit, and for what reason? To protect the children. Fuck the children. Give the little fuckers a good hard dose of reality. Why do you think that Columbine shit happened? Not enough reality. And no, I don't blame video games for that. Granted, they needed more reality, but that "too much video gaming" thing isn't what I meant. What I meant was that whole Parental Involvement thing. Trust me, if Video Games made people go off, there would be a whole lot less motherfuckers reading this shit! There would be a whole lot less kids running around because most of you dipshits would have been killed off already. If you REALLY want to protect the children, prepare them for the hazards of life. Don't hide shit from them, they won't be prepared for it when shit goes down. Their little brains will seize up, and bang, they will die. Let them know it ain't safe to walk down the street. Maybe, just maybe, when little Donald walks to his friend's house, he'll stay alert long enough to spot the asshole who wants to steal his allowance to feed his crack habit!

If I was a parent of say, a 7th or 8th grader, you know, that age where Halloween was still FUN! Assume for a moment, that I am the parent of twins this age. Those kids would be wearing some matching, but custom made costumes. Oh yeah. And you are going to say, "You wouldn't send your kid to school like that." Bet your ass I would. And I'd have my girlfriend right with me. Just goading me on. Bet your ass on that. The costume(s) I'm talking about are the twin towers of the WTC. Oh yeah. No shit. I said it. I'd dress my kids up with home made costumes of the WTC. Not only that, but each kid(tower) would have a plane sticking out of it. Maybe even toss in some army-men(the 2-3 inch tall plastic jobs) painted to look like civilians going to work. Just so they could fling them off the "roof" of the costume. Maybe if we put the fun back into childhood, maybe those kids wouldn't be shooting up the schools. Or even be shooting up IN the schools!

Back and Forth, is that a bass-ackward statement or what? This is a classic case of street American. Were this REAL English, it would be Forth and Back, in the order in which the events occur. Of course, we run against the global-grain on many things...this being one of them.

Remember, you can't come back, until you've gone forth.

I've always been a proponent of switching the drinking age, and the driving age. Let's face one fact, no. Let's face SEVERAL facts. For one, teens are going to drink. And by keeping it a "bad" thing, we are encouraging it, because it is representative of disregard for the establishment and the power structure. You can't stop teens from drinking anymore than you can stop an idiot on a bulldozer from tearing the shit out of a corn crop. He/she's going to do it if he/she wants to bad enough. Another thing, this would promote family bonding. Hey, someone would have to drop you off at the bar! Might as well be your parents. At least they would know where you were, and who you were with. That would make them feel better.

I know why Teenagers are so unhappy, Ignorance is Bliss, and they know everything.

Why do so many people have things "go in one ear and out the other"?? Because there is nothing inside to stop it, that's why!

Bald in NOT beautiful. It's not sexy, natural, or attractive. How many women do you see at the bar who are as bald on the head as a newborn on the ass, getting picked up by someone worth getting picked up by? NONE! Of course, I could say the same thing of the guys. And that short-hair shit came into fashion only about 150 years ago. Some people seem to think it means something special to keep your hair short if you are a guy. I remember one time, in one of those dollar/cheap as shit stores, that some little girl asked her mom "Why does that man have long hair?" Her mother didn't give a good answer, I forget what she said exactly, but it wasn't to my liking. I remember walking over to the kid, and asking her if she had ever heard of Jesus. She said that she had, and I remarked that Jesus Christ, her savior, had long hair. And noted that just because a man may have long hair doesn't make him a bad person. She understood what I meant, and her mother was pissed. She was pissed because I went against her norms, but gave a good enough argument to actually open her child's eyes. I let that kid know that all she knew may not be completely accurate, and actually may have given her a more valuable a lesson in life than any teacher she ever had.

"Planded" is the kind of word that lets you know that your brain has stopped functioning, but your mouth hasn't.

News programs are 95% entertainment and 5% informative.

Is ANYONE 100% sure that George W. Bush isn't a clone?

Picture this: George Carlin as President, Alice Cooper as Vice President, Ozzy Osborne as Speaker of the House, and Ted Nugent as Secretary of Defense/ Homeland Security. This will tell me that the people of this country are serious about straightening shit out.

Can someone please explain to me the difference between the Secretary of Defense and the Director of Homeland Security? If you actually look at the names, the Secretary looks like he would answer to the Director...but in my eyes, it seems as though these two both have the same job!

Would the world be a better place if Women were in charge? Maybe. I doubt it though, too much is fucked up. Besides, we know that women who live in the same abode together long enough, tend to synchronize(more proof of a female plot against men), meaning they all go on their period at the same time(this explanation brought to you by the "Mother Nature For Retards" line of books) this being the case, imagine if you will, 50,000 women in the military, all on the rag at the same time, ready to attack an enemy position. Looks to me like the side to PMS first would win!

And to those who want to say "America, Love it or Leave it."...please note, I'm trying to do the latter! Buy this book and I might be able to!

I hear there are some really great deals on land in Afghanistan right now.

Have you heard about the latest in medical warnings? That colo-rectal cancer scare they are tossing around? Get your ass checked out now, before it's too late! This almost seems like something a gay proctologist came up with to drum up some new business. Like I need to see this shit on TV while I'm eating my breakfast. Holy shit! I better go get that colo-rectal screening done before I forget. Drop the bowl of rice crispies, and run to the doctor so he can shove a camera up my ass. Maybe if he sticks it up there far enough, he can find out what I ate yesterday that upset my stomach and made me fart green clouds! Can't this shit be done on a regular check up? I mean, who the fuck is going to wait until you have a tumor hanging out of your ass to get checked out? "Honey, look! I grew a third testicle!" "No you didn't, either that's a huge hemorrhoid, or you have a tumor hanging out of your ass! You might want to get that checked out."

I came up with an idea. Actually, I come up with all kinds of ideas, but this one just might make me want to open up a hotel. It would be the only hotel in the world offering the "Lick-A-Breast Wake Up Call Service." Instead of just ringing the phone of the clientele who need to be woken up at a certain hour, our specialist will enter the room, and lick their breasts until they rouse from slumber. After all, nobody likes to wake up to the alarm, and it would be even worse with a fucking telephone ringing in your ear. Imagine being woken up by a pair of strange lips on your nipple. If that doesn't wake you the fuck up fast, nothing will. Not only that, but imagine the tips if the recipient enjoys the experience! And I bet hiring people for this task wouldn't be too hard.

I've pretty much seen everything. In Baltimore, Maryland several police higher-ups resigned over a departmental memo that went around. It seems as though a black male of unknown age and description committed several rapes in a small area of town. The memo suggested stopping(stopping, not arresting, but merely stopping and asking a few questions of) every black male around a certain spot until the rapist was found. This actually sounds like the police are trying to do their jobs for once. However, the "Racial Profiling" crowd went ballistic over this idea. I guess they would rather we allow the black rapist to run around loose, while whites and Hispanics, as well as every oriental person in town are stopped and questioned.

The leading cause of death, is birth. If you were born, chances are sometime down the line, you are going to die. It's a fact of nature.

Another health alert I've been hearing about, using rubbers when you masturbate. Who the fuck is dumb enough to believe they are going to catch something from their own penis? And to this point, I'd have to ask, would you put the rubber on your dick, or your hand? Maybe the really fucked up kids, the ones who are majorly paranoid, will put them on BOTH! I suppose the schizophrenics will argue about whether it's the hands responsibility, or the penis' responsibility to wear the protection.

Some bullshit job titles: Certified Nursery Specialist (for flowers!), Software Engineer(Programmer), Developmental Technologist(I have no clue what the fuck this could be, maybe Engineer?) Healthcare Provider(Another bullshit name for DOCTOR!)

Have you heard the latest from New York? Some woman is buying rakes and pitchforks for the NYFD to use for the sifting of the rubble of the WTC. And they are actually referring to them as "Recovery Tools." Is this going to be the new Standard Issue on fire trucks? I'm not making this up! I saw it on the news! What happens when Lowes and Home Depot run out? I can see them gathering up a fleet of 20-30 U-Haul pick-ups and driving to Kentucky and raiding the farmers. "What the Hell are you people DOING?!" "We're confiscating your Recovery Tools! We need them at Ground Zero! It's your patriotic duty to give these up!"

I once wrote a production; "Crackheads On Ice". But nobody bought it.

If I have managed to offend you in some way, please note: I'm not sorry.

Has anyone thought about this? The old Nazi SS and the US Secret Service have more in common than just the initials. If you think about it, it might come to you what I mean.

I saw something funny on the news this morning, someone with a pilots license was attempting to land their plane, a Cessna I believe, at an airfield in Ocean City, Md. And missed. But not by just a little bit... by half the fucking island! How the fuck can you completely miss the airfield, and think the wavy ocean below might be just as good?

Here's something I'm just waiting for, because I know it's coming. Once all the rubble has been removed from the WTC site, someone, somewhere, is going to refer to it as; "The Site Formerly Known as Ground Zero." I can feel it coming. And where did that whole Ground Zero thing originate? That term usually indicates where an atomic detonation took place. Seems to me that 220 floors of buildings collapsing is still slightly smaller in devastation than a nuclear device going off.

Here is something you never see on the evening news; During the report of a string of break-ins in a small neighborhood, some guy standing in front of his house yelling "YEAH! Let that motherfucker break into my motherfucking house. I'll bust a cap in dat nigga's motherfucking ass! Right here, this address, come on motherfucker, break into my motherfucking house! Punk ass bitch!"

I designed a T-Shirt: A tattered American flag on the front, with the legend "Every Empire Falls" scrawled across it. On the back, a list of all the great empires in the worlds history. You know, the ones who thought it would last forever. Just like Rome, America will someday fall. The funny part is, everyone is still on that "this country has lasted for 225+ years, through thick and thin" kick. I got a news flash for you, the Roman Empire lasted for several THOUSAND years. Got a long way to go to cover that territory.

Sports need a reworking for the 21st century. All the sports we know came from the last century, or before. We need some updates for this shit. And leave it to me to know how to make sports much more interesting. Baseball, what a boring fucking game. What do they have? 3 fights a year? What the fuck is that? Several changes come to mind for this, let's make it interesting. Two snipers on the upper deck. But they can only nail base stealers. That would make shit interesting. "Bob Tagget, on first, takes his lead off step, HE RUNS FOR IT! DASHING FOR SECOND BASE, OH! The right field upper deck sniper just took him down. Looks like he'll be missing the rest of this game." And let the batter keep the bat as he rounds the bases. I bet we won't be seeing so many double plays after that rule goes through. Football: This used to be a real manly sport. Then came the pads. Hey, Einstein, I got a flash for ya, women wear pads! Not men! And women only wear them once a month. You sissy-Mary candy asses wear them during practice, as well as the game! Mayhapse there be some gay thing going on the general populous doesn't know about? Be men, throw the helmets away, and take the chance. And let the fights go on as part of the game. Hell, if you get the lines set up, and two guys are still fighting, you might get an offsides penalty thrown on that. Basketball: More annoying shit. Either raise the fucking nets up five feet, or ban any player over six feet tall. And bring back the glass backboards! I used to love seeing those fuckers shatter and spray glass everywhere. Put the danger back into it.

What genius writes for the news anyway? I saw a story about a 14 year old girl who was breaking into houses and stealing all kinds of shit, to feed her mother's drug habits. Nice kid. Anyway, she was caught, but somehow managed to get away from the detention area she was being held at, and now the break-ins have started back up again. So the police and the media are asking for help to find this girl. If anyone sees her, call police immediately. Ok. Will do, but would you mind showing us a fucking picture of this bitch? "Hey Police, I saw a suspicious looking 14 year old girl today, might be the one from the news story. Couldn't really tell for sure though, no one showed us what she looked like. But Goddammit, she looked suspicious to me!"

I'd love to get in front of a psychiatrist. I can prove I'm sane. And I could probably drive him or her nuts proving it. They'd show me one of those ink-blot tests, and I'd have to be the smart-ass. "That looks really cool!" "What do you see?" "An ink blot." "What?" "I see an ink blot. Looks like someone cracked open a Bic Pen and shook it like hell. Hey, I like the pattern, but do you have one in another color? It would definitely look good in the den, but doesn't match the color scheme in there."

Homosexuals never, ever, go off on their co-workers. It doesn't happen. I'd like to see it happen once though, picture that, you call that guy a "fag" one too many times, and he leaves in a huff, runs down to the YMCA, grabs up a bunch of buddies, comes back, and they hold you down while your favorite whipping boy redecorates your office. Next thing you know, you've got lace curtains, a huge floral arrangement on your desk, and the pictures of your wife and kids have been replaced by a stack of "Men's Health" magazines. Then they take pictures of your new surroundings and post them on the alt.gaymenwhorunfortune500companies newsgroup.

I don't miss Connie Chung. That bitch wais more annoying than the theme song to "Friends".

I'm working on remixing a pair of songs; the words of 'Memories' from the "Cats" production, and the music of 'Through the Never' by Metallica. I think it might work. We'll find out.

Here's a topic you'll never see on those daytime talk shows; "Dykes who can rip one like a drunk truck driver."

Another one I *KNOW* you'll never see; "People whose lives are not fucked up in any way, shape, or form." Where would they find the guests? Never happen. Those people simply don't exist.

Have you ever taunted your car by driving it to a junkyard? The car starts giving you some trouble, so you take it to the junkyard and just drive around, musing to yourself, "Keep fucking with me, and you will end up here. You can be replaced with a much newer model." I highly recommend against pulling this stunt with your wife/girlfriend and the "Red-Light" district.

Speaking of junkyards, I once took a picture of a new looking car, and one of a severely sliced up junker(same models, and colors of course), and put them together, side by side. Under the new car, I put the legend "This is your body." And under the junker, I put "This is your body after the paramedics find the 'Organ Donor' part of your license is checked YES!"

If you think America isn't getting back to normal, I offer up this little bit of proof; I saw a woman driving a car, yammering on a cell phone, while in not one, but two of her car windows, I saw those "Baby on Board" signs. Now, we all know cell phones while driving are dangerous, and should be(and may soon be) illegal. But who the fuck is dumb enough to expect the rest of us to drive safer because her baby is in the car, while driving with a fucking cell phone?!

Someone needs to print up some Catholic Priest Scorecards, so we can keep a tract of who has molested the most kids, which church they have done so in, and maybe the church with the most molesters on file can win a free trip for the Bishop to go to the Vatican.

Speaking of those "proud parent" bumper stickers, if this isn't some of the most self righteous bullshit I've ever seen. I want to see a bumper sticker that reads "Embarrassed Child of Idiot Parents!"

Most people who are content with their life have their standards set way too low.

Tim Curry would make a great "Annie".

I put a speaker behind the grill in my truck. I ran it into my CB radio, so I can flip a switch, and be able to be heard for blocks. This is a good thing, it relieves road rage. It also has saved me a broken window. This little punk kid was standing on a street corner, tossing rocks at cars. The little moron wasn't even hidden! At least when I did that shit as a kid, they never knew where it came from! Anyway, I saw the fucker pick up a rock as I was approaching, and called out over my CB "BOY! YOU BETTER PUT THAT ROCK DOWN!" in a real deep voice. He stiffened up, and had this look on his face like the voice of God spoke to him. After I passed, I saw his hand open up, and a rock the size of his 7 year old fist dropped to the ground. I hope I scarred that retard for life.

Whatever happened to the Guardian Angels? Curtis Sliwa and that ugly fucking sister of his. Not that I'm too anxious to see them again, but they've been very quiet since the late 80's. Big fucking newsmakers for about 8 months, then dropped off the face of the Earth. Where were they on Sept. 11?

I want to see someone introduce "Street Olympics". This could be fun. Think about it, the 100 Meter Mugging! That would be great for a cities morale! Another event could be the Pass the Purse Relay Race(instead of that queer looking baton). Hell, they could start the races by shouting "FREEZE! PUT DOWN THAT TELEVISION!" Instead of the old

"Ready, Set..." But keep the gun. You gotta have a gunshot to start the race. It's appropriate.

There is a new show on worth watching, Hallelujah! It's called "The Osbornes". If you don't know who OZZY is, you need to die. Plain and simple. All I can say about this show, is that I thought *I* had a dysfunctional life! The show rocks, Ozzy rules, and I love it!

Something else I've started doing, and you with the cell phones can thank whichever company came up with the stupid commercial for it, but now I yell out "CAN YOU HEAR ME NOW?!" When I encounter one of you nits.

I have also figured out why they call our president "W." For short....because the word starts with "DUH!" DUH-BYA. Yep, it's appropriate. And in case you haven't put two and two together, he's actually the second George W. to be president and fuck things up. The first was Washington. I can't really bitch too much about Washington, at least he grew pot!

If, at this point, I have not offended you, please note, I'll get to it.

There's been a lot of shit going on in the Middle East lately, Palestinians blowing themselves up in Israel, Israeli troops attacking neighborhoods in Palestinian Territory "looking for terrorists", all kinds of shit going on. And have you noticed that it's never called Palestine, but a territory. The name smacks of political bullying. Terrorist, territory, they sound oddly similar. The UN steals land from the Palestinians, gives it to the Jews, calls it Israel, and everyone wonders why the Palestinians are pissed off about it? Suppose the government came in, took half of your yard, gave it to someone you hate, and told you that you couldn't do anything about it. How the fuck would you feel? And do you know how they came up with the name Israel? Look at the word, IS REAL(Ok, flip the A and the E), probably started out as IT'S REAL. Not to the Palestinians it ain't! It's bullshit! It's theft. So let's change the name to Istheft. It even sounds more religious.

Can someone explain to me why, when it's done against America, or someone we support politically, we call it Terrorism. Yet when someone we support does it against someone we don't, they call it Guerilla Warfare by Freedom Fighters?

Something else I've noticed about that whole Israeli thing, they've been bitching about what the Nazi's did to them for over 50 years now. Looks to me like they are doing the same fucking thing to the Palestinians. Raiding towns, separating men from their families, torturing and killing at will, and justifying it with this whole anti-terrorism thing going around. You want to get rid of terrorism once and for all, stop fucking with these people! Stop supporting their enemies! Let them deal with it! Stay the fuck out of their affairs! America can play peacemaker and tell other countries how to take care of their own, when we can't even do it for ourselves? Where is the logic in this argument? Oh, I get it, those who can't, teach.

After watching some of the clips from the speeches of the 2K2 Oscars, it thrills me to know that education isn't lost on movie stars. And yes, for those of you who are dense, there was sarcasm dripping from that statement.

Am I the only one who's noticed that most movies have the best parts in the trailer? Especially here lately. It seems as though you see all the best stuff in the trailer, and that all the scenes that connect those together are what really make these movies suck.

For those of you wondering, I use 2K2 for the year because I got tired of that Y2K shit, and this is my revenge. Y2K this, Y2K that, we're all gonna die on Y2K. Yeah, we're all dead all right. Blame all that shit on Gates. Yeah, why couldn't he be the real life Mr. Bill.

Any of you who don't know who Mr. Bill was should be shot.

I heard more interesting stuff in the news lately, the Cartoon network will no longer be showing Speedy Gonzales cartoons. Why? Because it's insensitive to Mexicans. O-Kay, I can see that, he's a superfast mouse, who outsmarts the big mean cat all the time, gets whatever he wants, and this is offensive. I understand this. If I was a stupid lazy motherfucker, and was being portrayed that way, I'd be offended too.

The Catholic Church really IS Satan's whore. Deal with it.

I want to start a whole new thing, Mini-Dog Fights. You've heard of Cock-Fights, Pit-Bull fights(and I'll get to Pit Bulls shortly), Dobies(I said DOBIES, not DOOBIES!), Rotts, Sheps, all these dogs get a bad rap. It's time to get some real shit started! Imagine one of those Tea-Cup Poodles whipping the shit outta a Pekinese! That would be funny as shit!

Big dogs are cool, it's been my experience that they are really sweethearts. It's them little fucking dogs with the Napoleon Complex that are the trouble makers! Them and the idiots who teach those big dogs to fight. They make them mean. Not only that, but all that inbreeding, shit, look what inbreeding has done to the south! You think it doesn't fuck with a dogs DNA? Of course it does.

A fact known throughout the world, except in America: 98% of American breweries produce junk. There are a few micro-brews worth drinking, but all of the major brands are laughed at throughout the world. It is a fact. Deal with it.

I am a male lesbian, and damned proud of it.

It's spelled LEIF, but pronounced layph. Get it right, or shut the fuck up.

You know something I do when I'm driving? When I pull up to a red-light on a multilane street, I look for who is going to go the fastest when the light turns green. I get behind them. You ever do that? Probably not. I figure it has never occurred to you. But I do it, I never end up behind a school bus, trash truck, or anyone with a "Proud Parent" bumper sticker. I hate being slowed down when I'm running late. And I gotta tell you, there isn't a vehicle on the road with a faster take-off than me. No one gets the better of me at a red light. Doesn't happen. I refuse to let it. I fucked with a cop one time, we were both in the lead position, and I took off like a bat out of hell. Flew up to the speed limit, and stayed there. It's not illegal, there is no law on the books that says you have to take 30 minutes to reach the speed limit(take note of this, most of you DO take 30 minutes to reach the speed limit!) So I get there as fast as possible. If there is a cop around, I hang right at that speed limit. And don't fucking tailgate me. I hate that shit. It pisses me off, because I am a whole lot smarter than you are, and I know where the cops sit to give out ransom tickets. If I'm doing the speed limit, there is a speed trap nearby. Bet on it. I have on occasion done two things, depending on my mood. Either I slow down to 10 MPH below the speed limit, or I pull over and let you fucking pass me. Sometimes

I do both, so you get nice and pissed off before you go flying into that money trap. I've gotten several people quite pissed off and then pulled over right before the speed trap. They go flying by, race up to 60 MPH, and I pass them within a minute while Officer Friendly is giving them a lecture on the necessity of obeying the speed limit, while writing out that ticket. I usually smile and wave as I pass them. Being that I am such a naturally friendly human being.

Just imagine if Porky Pig had sang the opening theme to The Jeffersons.

Something else I want to see, Tractor Trailer Chicken. This could be a real neat new game show.

The only thing that makes me want to get frozen when I die is so I can see just how fucked up the world is really going to get before the Earth strikes back!

2002 is going to go down as the "Year of the Pedophile Priests."

I remember one time when I was tripping, I saw a smiley face dead center in the toilet bowl. It tried to bite my dick off when I started peeing on it. Fortunately, it missed and didn't get it. I almost laughed my ass off when my girlfriend suggested taking a shit on the smiley face, and giving him a brown hat to wear. I got a visual of the smiley face wearing a pile of shit for a hat. After a while, when I didn't see the smiley face anymore, we reasoned that Mr. Hanky came and took the smiley face away for wearing a turd hat without being in the union.

If you somehow don't believe that I am the person your parents warned you about, you need to be bitch slapped.

My mind is a very dangerous place to be. That is why I spend so much time out of it. It's not safe in there, I know it. Way too much going on in my head for me to deal with. I'd rather let it do it's thing, while I go out and have a good time.

I once knew a guy who had more personalities than there are players in the NFL. He was a major source of entertainment during my 20's. He was on several kinds of medications for it, and we'd hide them frequently. You can't imagine how that affected his entertainment value. Took it right off the scale. I forget his name, but he was one fucked up individual.

For those of you who watch South Park, I know the real Butters. I thank God that I'm not that pathetic. Two hits, three beers, and he's done.

It's a shame this guy's dead, he was a scream. I worked with him for a few years, his name was John, but we called him JR. Great guy when he was sober, but a laugh-a-minute when he was fucked up. He had a kinda epileptic thing, it wasn't exactly epilepsy, but he would have seizures. He'd get all fucked up on greeners, liquor, weed, pcp, you name it, and go into "Jesus Mode". He got a little too obnoxious at a party one time, so I took my handcuffs off my jeans, and we slapped them on him, and tossed him in the back of a pickup truck. After he settled down, he went into Jesus Mode, and told us, "I'm Jesus Christ, and I love you all, BUT, you're all going to Hell anyway." The worst part was, he became so incoherent that he couldn't tell us where he lived. I got the address off of his ID, but it was his parents' house. We dropped him off at 3:15 am, fortunately, his parents didn't know any of us. They weren't happy. I thought they should have been, at least we made sure he was safe.

I have lots of fucked up friends. I always did. This is a good thing. It makes you appreciate how good things are for you. My life has been one seriously fucked up mess, but it could be worse. I know this for a fact, and I have the friends to prove it.

Americans are way too uptight about sex. It's not a good thing to show a naked breast on TV, but showing a guys brain splattered all over the pavement is. I think there should be more sex on TV. Or maybe that would offend the people who are too ugly to get any. We can't go around offending people. Especially the ugly ones. Like they aren't offensive enough themselves!

Just what the fuck is a "Room Parent" in a school? What happened to the teacher? Oh, right, teachers teach, and these kids don't get educated, they get programmed, like a computer. Maybe they should call them "Pediogrammers".

I had an interesting thing happen in Rite Aid today, the clerk asked me if I wanted to donate a dollar to some charity, and write my name on a slip of paper that they hang in the window. I told him that "I'll donate a dollar when they start paying my bills." He seemed quite taken aback by this. Then he offered "But if you donate a dollar, you get eight dollars in coupons." Now, my mind began doing the math on that. If I donate one dollar, and get eight dollars back, who is donating the other seven dollars to me? So I said, "How can they afford to do that?" His reply was not unexpected, "I don't know." I pressed the issue. "And why doesn't whoever is giving the money for the coupons just donate that money, and stop bothering us working people?" Apparently, this concept never occurred to him. I was bothered by the fact that a lot of people buy into this scheme. "Oooooooooooooh, look at me, my name is on a piece of paper, I'm a great fucking humanitarian!" I'm not against charities, but give me a fucking break! Donate, and be fucking quiet about it. Don't do it for the recognition, that shows me that you are a shallow, self centered asshole, who needs a brick jammed in your ear.

Reality TV, this shit has really GOT TO FUCKING GO! Have you heard about the latest? The Bachelor? What kind of pathetic shit is this anyway? Twenty five sluts living with one ugly, desperate, sorry sumbitch who probably couldn't get laid in a whorehouse. How fucking desperate are these women? Has the bar scene become so bad that women feel the need to go on TV and beg for a fucking husband? Jesus

Christ, go on a blind date or something, anything is better than embarrassing yourself on TV looking like a desperate tramp.

I've heard about Secretary's Day, excuse me, "Professional Administrative Assistant's" day. How about "Lazy Bitch's Day", my girlfriend would like that one. In fact, she came up with it.

Having a smoking section in a restaurant is like having a pissing section in a swimming pool.

I'm a smoker, and isn't it bad enough that we've been taxed unfairly, and been segregated from the rest of the populous? Not only do we still have those anti-smoking fucks on our asses, but now some group of them gets together to tell us "Infect Truth!". Read this book motherfucker, I'm infecting truth. Not just political bullshit to raise taxes and service my own agenda, but I'm giving it all to ya. You bastards are just plain annoying. Why don't you all get together with MADD and have a jack-off-a-thon.

Ever wonder what Carrie Fisher would say to Natalie Portman? Something like, "Hi Mom!"

Whoever said "History Never Repeats" apparently didn't live in the 90's. We went thought the 60's, a quick blast of the 70's, and now we're back in the '80s. All in one decade! Thankfully, that 70's part didn't last too long. Disco was bad enough the first time around! I always said, that those who reminisce about the 70's didn't live through them. And I was right about that. A lot of 80's metal bands are touring again, this is a cool thing actually. I got stuck in the 80's, did take a little trip back to the 60's during the early 90's, but not for more than a summer. But I haven't changed a whole lot since the 80's. I got the long hair, a couple of tattoos, which I got in 2K1, but still, I've had that whole 80's attitude the whole time. I think I'll even pull out my ripped jeans this summer, just to make a statement.

Speaking of the ripped jeans, I still can't believe that there were posers out there who paid upwards of $300 a pair for them. I made my own. A few razor cuts, toss some bleach on them, wash them a few times, and whammo. Some dude in a grocery store one time stopped me and asked me where I had gotten them. I figured he was too lame to find out you could do them yourself, so I told him I had ordered them from California, and that they cost me $400. I was not the least bit surprised when he replied, "Damn, man, that's CHEAP!" Only a poser......

I heard that the same station that did "The Bachelor" is thinking of doing the reverse, "The Bachellorette". One woman, in a house, with twenty five men. Doesn't this too closely resemble the bar scene? One woman, twenty five desperate fucks who can't get a date, and she has to eliminate them from contention for her attention. If that isn't Friday Night at the Singles Bar, I don't know what is. The ratio sounds about right, too.

Somehow, somewhere along the line, you may have gotten the idea that I can be a very violent person. You are right.

Men, I want you to remember something, there are women out there who still remember Lorena Bobbit, and what she did. And who would probably do a bit worse. You should realize that you may be married to one of those women. You also won't really know, for sure, until they've done it to you. Actually, John Bobbit was a lucky bastard. My girlfriend would have stuck that thing in a blender and purre'd that motherfucker. In all fairness to her, she probably would have done something like this after that; "If you want your dick back, you'll have to drink this. Drink it, and it's yours." Slick way of disposing of the evidence, making you drink your own penis. Won't have to worry about sewing that sucker back on.

What happens if a funeral procession goes through a red light, that's legal if the hearse went through a green or yellow. But what if the following cars go through a red light with a camera there? Do they still get the ticket? Probably. But, doesn't that beg the question, couldn't you use that as an excuse to get out of the ticket? Even if you aren't in a funeral? Just say that you were, there was no cop present, and no one to argue against you. Just cry a lot, and say how unjust it is that you get a ticket while burying uncle Bob.

I saw something today that made me feel much safer. Baltimore City is a "Nuclear Free Zone." I feel very secure knowing that anyone who brings a nuclear device into this town is going to be prosecuted to the fullest extent of the law. I just hope we can send the police after someone who detonates one above the city. Wouldn't that be a fucking hoot? Someone nukes Baltimore, and a few days later, a cop comes knocking on their door to arrest them. But speaking of the legalities of bringing nuclear shit into Baltimore, I wonder if all those doctors at John's Hopkins are going to get arrested now.

I just thought of something, they don't dare film "The Bachelorette" during the fall, when football is on. That woman would learn real quick what kind of mistake that shit is. She'd be trying to get their attention, and the only way she'd get any at all is to keep the beers coming and the chip bowls full. And God help her if she stood in front of that TV.

I used to work in a liquor store, and believe me, I've seen idiots at their prime! Like one time this guy walked in, I'm standing behind the counter, and he walks around in front of it, and asks me with a straight face, "Do you work here?" My reply was "No, I'm holding up the joint, but decided to be nondescript by waiting on customers." He was like, "Really? Should I leave so you can finish?" There was only one answer to that; "Would you mind? I'd really hate for the cops to show up before I get it all." He left. I just stood there shaking my head. He must have thought I stole the video surveillance tape, cuz the cops never showed up.

Now I work at a Florist. What a change, going from dealing with miserable fucks looking to get loaded, to filling orders for miserable fucks trying to get forgiveness from their girlfriend/wife/mistress/ etc... Guys, let me give you some advice, if you piss her off, flowers you didn't pick, and a note you didn't write, aren't going to work. And I see the messages you want me to write, "I'm sorry I'm such an ass. - Love Bob". One of these days I'm going to do some creative editing on those notes. And let me tell you, the cheesiest fucking note I've seen yet, was actually a change. It was originally "Thank you for the best weekend of my life! - All my love, Pete" But 'Pete' decided to change it, to something just as pathetic, "This is only the beginning! - Love, Pete" Now, either this sumbitch got lucky over the weekend, or he wants everyone to THINK he got lucky over the weekend. Either way, this was NOT an appropriate thing to do. Thank the woman in person for God's sake, and if you were any good, she'd be sending YOU flowers and a sappy note. And speaking of that, working at a florist, I've seen how rotten you women can be too. Sending a guy a dozen red roses in a box, with a huge balloon, "Happy Anniversary! I LOVE YOU!" And all that happy stuff. And sending it to his work! You know Goddamned well he's going to catch the shit from his coworkers. Personally, if I was a woman, and I did that shit, I'd make sure the card read "Thanks for the most incredible weekend of my entire life! -Love Fred!" Hey, if you're going to do it ladies, DO IT FUCKING RIGHT! Really embarrass that sumbitch. Hell, if he gets pissed off about it, don't fuck him for a month. That'll straighten his attitude out. He'll learn how to take a fucking joke.

Unlike most of you, I actually DO understand what Ozzy is saying.

Anyone who truly believes that "The customer is always right" have never had to deal with them.

If those Sylvan Learning Center teachers are so good, why aren't they teaching the public school teachers the secret?

I went to see a band called "Crack The Sky" at Baltimore's Inner Harbor, just so happens, that was on 4-20...the band kicked ass, as they always do. But oddly enough, on 4-20, not one single whiff of pot came floating by. What the fuck is wrong with you people? It's national marijuana day, you lame fuckers attend a live concert, and DON'T BLAZE UP!? It was mostly older motherfuckers at the show, those that were in their prime during the hippy times, and none of you people had a fucking joint!? What a waste of flesh you've become. And another thing, just to show how pathetic you people have become, I saw a guy there, who was holding up a cell phone so the person on the other end could hear the show. It's not bullshit, I saw it with my own eyes.

For those keeping score, I've used the word "fuck" or some derivative thereof a total of 179 times so far.

I know I keep using the term "Today", but realize, that I wrote this book over the course of a year, and a lot of things I put in were referenced to that day.

Today, I made an arrangement of a dozen roses in a vase, it looked good, of course, those are simple, I could do that in my sleep. Anyway, I went to fill out the card and envelope, and read the card I was to write, and I swear, it read "Love is rare, and hard to find. Keep taking off your pants, and we'll be fine." I was like, WHOA! Some dude is looking to not get laid for a year! Was I wrong...it was being sent TO a guy! At work! By a chick! Now this goes back to that whole "Rotten shit women do to embarrass us men." I'm telling you, that fucked with my head for about 5 minutes. I tell you the truth, after thinking about it, I would rather have been the delivery driver when he got that. The look on that face HAD to be priceless. And worst of all, you know that poor motherfucker was in for it from his coworkers. That's the kind of shit you just don't live down. He'll be hearing about it for months!

Guys, know something, women have us by the nuts, and they know it. Never fuck around with your woman. Treat her right, and she'll be yours forever. Don't, and she'll tell all her friends, and when word spreads, you'll be dating your hand for the rest of your sad pathetic life.

For those who were dumb enough to go back and count how many times I used the word "fuck" or some derivative thereof, I lied. I just wanted to make you go back and count them, and I have to wonder how many times you counted, thinking you missed a few. And yes, I am a rotten motherfucker for that.

The Moral Majority can kiss my ass.

Those of you who think I am a sexist pig, you couldn't be farther from the truth. I am a lesbian with a penis. There aren't many of us out there, most men are idiots who actually do think with their dicks, when they can be bothered to think at all. I just happen to know the simple truths about people. If you don't like it, tough.

Speaking of simple people, what the fuck is wrong with all of you, anyway? I've started reading the warning labels on products recently...like the one I saw on deodorant for crying out loud, "If a rash appears, discontinue use." Ok, who really would rub something in a particular place on their body, and if a rash appears, NOT think what you are rubbing on it MIGHT be the cause? How about this one on a chain saw; "Caution- Blade is sharp" No shit, well let me dull that fucker down so I won't get hurt! "Warning- Do NOT touch moving blade!" Well fuck me. How am I suppose to find out if it's sharp enough to cut down a tree if I don't touch it when it's moving? What a fucking surprise, a device meant to cut wood, and it has a SHARP blade. Who'dathunkit? And the worst part of this whole warning label thing, is that someone, somewhere, had to do something that stupid and sue the manufacturer. Like that stupid fuck who sued McDonalds for their own fucking mistake, putting a cup of steaming hot coffee between their legs. Use the cup holder for crying out loud. And you can thank Christ I wasn't on that jury. If I had been, I'd have your picture taken and made into a poster with the caption "I'm a retard who burned my crotch because I'm stupid, and I didn't get any money out of the deal." And I heard about some stupid woman who lit a cigarette, while in an oxygen tent. One less retard in the gene pool. If only more stupid people would commit suicide in these ways, there would be a whole lot less trouble in this world.

You really want to know how Patriotic people were after Sept. 11, and personally, I think this is going a little far, but I saw a mugger wearing a ski mask done up like the American flag. And after he mugged the guy, he ran off yelling, "IT'S GOING TO FIGHT THE TALIBAN!"

If you really want to piss off a car dealership, ask to test drive all of the cars that are blocked in. They have to give you a test drive. You make like you are actually interested in buying it, but they don't have to know you are just there to fuck with them.

Leno always gets a laugh, of course, it's usually HIS OWN!

Have you ever actually watched the American version of Weakest Link? I don't remember the hosts name, but if he isn't in the running for "Dork of the Year", then the contest is rigged! Anyway, I was channel surfing the other day, and ran across this show. I watched as players introduced themselves, and was struck by a funny occurrence. First, there was this really fat chick, then some chick who gave her name, and her occupations. Weight Loss Consultant(fat farm manager), and Caterer. Isn't that kinda like being an E.M.T. who works part time as a funeral director? Am I the only one who sees a conflict of interest here?

Let me take a survey here, women first, does your man treat you the way you feel you should be treated? Yes or no. All right, Men, do you treat your woman the way she should be treated? Yes or no, and don't be asking her! What the fuck is wrong with you? She's going to tell you "no!" What? Are you fucking retarded? Guys, never ask a woman for an answer to a question like that. She will tell you(maybe, maybe she'll tell you) "Yes dear, you treat me with all the TLC you can muster." But think about this, she's probably told all of her best friends what a rotten bastard you are. And it's probably true. Men don't treat women like they should. Well, some of us do. Not many though. Most men want their penis worshipped, and that's all they care about. Ok, let's take a page out of the bible. Jesus was worshipped, and he got nailed to a cross. Men, do you REALLY want your penis worshipped now? If you do, you are a sicker motherfucker than I am! You gotta take care of your woman. Don't get loaded and take shit out on her, it isn't her fault your life is fucked up, it's YOUR fault your life is fucked up. I know men don't take good care of their women, because the divorce rate is so fucking high. Of course, much like my theory of life, my theory of marriage holds up. The leading cause of divorce, is marriage. If you didn't get married, you couldn't get divorced. And don't bring up that shit about that moron kid who divorced her parents. That little shit doesn't count.

Speaking of marriage, I always wanted to get married in a graveyard. I figure if marriage is the death of bachelorhood, at least we'd be in a convenient place to bury it.

You know something I do in the waiting room of a doctor, excuse me, "healthcare provider", but what I do is this...I wait a maximum of 15 minutes past my appointment time, then I pull out my duck call. There ain't no law against tooting a duck call in a doctors office waiting room. For those of the denser persuasion, think of the sound a duck call makes.....QUACK,

QUACK! If I need to explain any further, please feel free to drown yourself.

You know your child is going to be a tough sumbitch, when right after it's born, it reaches up and yanks out the afterbirth. Musta been thinking something like "Where the fuck is my pillow?!"

Definitely a possibility....ok, which is it? Is it definite? Or just a possibility?

What the fuck is wrong here? The fire department runs hoses into the Chesapeake Bay to pump water onto a large fire at a mulch plant. Less than a week later, there is a large fire in a salvage yard, and the fire chief says on TV, "It's gonna take 3-4 days for it to burn itself out." Am I the only one who thinks a burning field of cars is what should be doused ASAP? If you are going to leave one burn, make it the non-toxic one!

Recently, here in Baltimore, a 16 year old moron "accidentally" killed his 12 year old brother by towing the dumb shit behind his parents pick up truck, in a plastic Oscar Mayer wienermobile made for a 6 year old. Both of these nits should have been wearing helmets, and I don't mean during this stupid stunt.

Anyone who would want to tow a 12 year old down the street in a plastic car at 30 miles an hour(about 29.5 MPH past the toys' design limits) NEEDS to wear a helmet! ALL THE FUCKING TIME! I'd almost be willing to bet that the parents of these retards try to sue the toy company, for failing to advise children to not to use the toy in such a manner. As a side note, always remember that if you lose control of your wiener, it can kill you.

You know something you just don't see, and I think we should start this one: A bunch of white guys standing on a street corner using the term "Cracka" on each other. "Man, what's wrong with your cracka ass?" "Don't be calling me a cracka, you cracka!" "Fuck your cracka ass, you cracka bitch!" I bet the niggers would go nuts if they saw that. Especially if they are all dressed in tan chinos with those ridiculous looking white sweaters with the alligator on the chest.

And don't get on my ass about using the word "Nigger". Fuck you. Blacks have turned that from a racial slur into a slang term. It's no big deal anymore. Besides, if your best friend can call you a nigger, and you won't get offended, why should a complete stranger using the term and not directing it at you, mean anything? Unless you are a complete moron, this shouldn't bother you.

On July 4th, Great Britain celebrates "Good Riddance Day!"

There really needs to be more concentration on parking during Drivers Ed...and during the actual driving test. Also, behavior on a parking lot should be emphasized. First of all, don't park in the handicap spots if you aren't handicapped. If you don't have a physical problem with your legs, you don't need the fucking spot. And don't park across more than one spot in an attempt to keep your new car nice looking. I target you assholes. I'll either get the aid of some like minded people and block your ass in, leaving just enough space to get through if you aren't really concerned about your paint job, or I'll just key your car. Another thing, don't park 1 foot in front of or behind my vehicle on a street. I have no compunction about banging into both cars that block me in. I have enough horse power to push you out of the way. If I don't have enough space to easily get out, I'll make it. And I don't care about your car, and have enough knowledge to repair any damage done to my own. It's old, paid for, and I don't give a fuck. Another thing about the parking lot thing, I love people who "love their cars"...let me relate an incident from about a month ago, I was on a Wal-Mart parking lot, and some black cunt pulls into the handicap spot next to me, gets out and starts walking towards the store(not hobble, limp, or ride on a "scooter" ...in other words, without needing to be in that spot,) stops, and calls out to some dickhead in a hotrod, who proceeds to back up, and bullshit with her. Needless to say, I was blocked in by this action. Now, I have the handicap tag for my grandmother, who is over 80 years old, and doesn't get around so well anymore. I started fuming, threw the truck into reverse, and started backing up. The dumbass in the hotrod spotted me, threw it into reverse, and just barely got out of my way. As I shifted into drive, I hollered out the window, "I didn't know being black was a handicap!" They both threw me a dirty look, but apparently knew better than to fuck with me.

How come when you fart in the shower after soaping up, you not only don't blow bubbles, but the fart still stinks?

Here's something I really want to see; one day on the news, when the interviewer is in the studio, and the interviewee is in "The Field"(and why do they call it "The Field", when it's in the middle of the fucking city?), have the interviewer ask a question, and have the reply be...."You're a nosey fucker aren't you?"

Have you seen those Target commercials? The ones with the blue outfits with the targets all over them? I say those outfits need to have every target on them bulls-eyed with a fucking shotgun! Where's Al-Qaeda when you fucking need them?!

Everytime I see a Dell commercial, and I hear that line "Dude! You're getting a Dell!" I respond with, "Dude! You need a bullet in the head!"

Something that just came out, Baltimore Police chief Ed Norris used a "secret fund" to look for another job. For those of you who think Baltimore is such a wonderful place, understand that even the POLICE CHIEF is looking to get the fuck out!

I saw a commercial this morning for some car dealer, they were having a "Super Slasher Sale"....and I wonder, how come doctors, surgeons, and lawyers don't have these kinds of sales? Wouldn't that be appropriate? "Are you having a kidney removed? Come on down now for our Super Slasher Sale, and for every kidney we remove at full price, we'll remove the other one for only $2.99!!!!" Wouldn't you run right on down and get this done? And think of the lawyer commercials..."Did you hack up more than one victim? Does the case look hopeless? Come on down to our law offices and check out the Super Slasher Sale we are having!"

I saw on the news where some guy got arrested in Canada, and this will show you just how fucked up the world really is, he got arrested for using a lighter to burn a long thread off of his sneakers. Ok, maybe some people are still taking that September 11 shit too seriously.

Isn't Barry Manilow dead yet?

Back when I was working at the liquor store, I saw something that really made me wonder about the idiocy of the American Public. I was between customers, and had to stay at the front of the store, so I'm looking out the front door. As I'm watching, two cars, one following the other, pulls up to the front door, with one person in each car. They pull up next to each other, and both are using cell phones. I saw one talking, then the other laugh, and then say something. When the second person stopped talking, the first one started laughing.

I watched this scene for about 10 minutes, and for the life of me, couldn't get over the fact that they were sitting next to each other, and talking to each other on cell phones!! It was just about closing time, and I was actually hoping they would keep talking until I locked the doors. Finally they hung up, and came in the store. I asked if they were talking to each other, and they admitted that they indeed were! I couldn't help but to make asses out of them both, someone needed to point this absurdity out to them. They laughed at what I had to say, but to this day I can't figure out why they were actually sitting in two cars, bullshitting with each other, and sitting no more than 6 feet away from each other!

Pop Quiz: Find the stupidity in the following quote. "Don't throw things into the storm drains, it goes right into the bay...eventually." -Bob Turk; weatherman on Baltimore's WJZ-13 station.

Ragweed, it's a pollen that a lot of people suffer an allergy from...to me, it sounds more like bad pot.

We were denied from getting a credit card, because I've had some problems in the past. When I called the credit card agency, and they told me that I was a delinquent payer, I mentioned that we were "co-conspirators, intent on stimulating the economy."

You know you've got a real classy woman, when she burps after giving you head.

I hear they are installing lap belts and shoulder restraints in school busses, in an effort to "protect the children." Now, can you imagine this? All it will take is one kid, just one, to refuse to put these things on, and that bus isn't going anywhere. And if it does, that driver is going to get fired.

Ray Hanania, a Palestinian-American comedian, who was billed to open for Jackie Mason, a Jewish comedian, was cancelled from opening the show because of the fact that he is a Palestinian. Someone is making a little bit of a stink over this, but the conflict seems to still be sedate. Had the roles been reversed, every Jew in the world would be screaming ANTI-SEMETISM, and gotten this guy blackballed from ever working a club again. And where is the ACLU now? Guess cuz the guy is more of an off-white, rather than black, they aren't interested.

We laughed our asses off the other morning. During one of the morning shows, we heard the intro to a commercial... "Some members of our studio audience will receive...." As the lead in for the sponsor...who's opening line was... "Every surgery is different..." I have no idea who the sponsor was, but we laughed so hard, we missed the next 10 minutes of the show.

Note to Priests: when I said "fuck the children" earlier, I meant it figuratively, not literally.

You never see those old Tarzan movies on TV anymore. I found out why, because the ACLU(Actually Clueless Losers Union) decided that the scantily clad natives are offensive to blacks. My question is... HOW?!?! I'd bet dimes to dollars that if you go to any jungle in Africa, there are people dressed like that. Guess what "homey", that's where you came from. Well, not YOU per say, but your people. And I got news for you, they don't hunt with Glocks and Tech-9s either! They hunt with fucking bamboo blowguns, bows and spears. Try doing one of your drive bys with a fucking blowgun! That kinda shit takes SKILL! Something you spray and pray nimrods wouldn't have a clue about. How can blacks be offended by this shit? And I bet most of you aren't. Hell, if I knew I came from a proud people(well, I do actually), who had lots of skills like that(they could survive with next to nothing!) I'd be one proud motherfucker. Ok, so they don't have cell phones, crack pipes, and welfare, I don't see this as a problem. These bastards know how to survive.

You never see a Pigmy with a hair-lip in those movies either. I looked.

Hey, lets all do something bizarre, call up your local "Alternative" music station(how they can call it alternative these days, with it being the most popular, hence, making it pop music, is beyond me,) but call them up, and request "Come Sail Away" by Styx. Just keep calling, and tell them it's as alternative as it gets.

Body language is a crock of shit. I sit or stand any way that makes me comfortable. And I don't mean feeling all happy-happy, joy-joy, either. I mean that if you see my arms folded in front of me, or on my hips, don't read anything into it, I'm centering my balance. The only time body language means anything in my case is when I'm about to beat the shit out of someone. Then I take a predatory stance.

I took a part time evening job at Fed-Ex, and let me tell you, putting a "Fragile: Handle with care" sticker on a package is like putting on a KKK sheet and walking down Baltimore Street alone at 2:30 am. Not a real smart idea. And we have this guy over there, he's one of the supervisors. His name is "irrelevant, and you aren't going to believe this shit, but I swear it's true, he looks like Irkle(the dorky black kid from "Family Matters"), and he talks like Irkle with a gay lisp. In fact, we were calling him Irkle for a while, but then I noticed something, he acts a lot like Tweek from South Park. In case you don't watch South Park(and if you don't...you need therapy for reading this book and not watching that show!) Anyway, Tweek is really high strung, his infamous line is "JESUS CHRIST! TOO MUCH PRESSURE! AAAHHHHH!" He doesn't actually say that, but he runs around and acts like those words are right on the tip of his tongue. So, in typical fashion, I combined Tweek and Irkle, and dubbed him "Twirkle". And that's been his name ever since. Spread like wildfire through the whole place.

There are thousands of people out there who would say I'm not right in the head. There are a lot of people out there who would say I *AM* right in the head.

And they would all make this claim for the SAME REASONS!

Speaking of Irkle, Twirkle, and dorks in general, I had the idea to take a "Whack-A-Mole" game and put Dork heads in place of the Moles...I mean, after all, what harm have moles done? They are just blind rodents who tunnel under ground and live a happy, uncomplicated life. Dorks have fucked up the world with all their technology. Look at Bill Gates for a prime example. Put those heads on that game and call it "Whack-A-Dork". Make the world safe for decent people.

Do you remember those cheesy insults from when you were a kid? Those "Your Momma" jokes? I hit someone recently with one, a new one; "Your momma looks like Yule Brenner in the morning." That stopped the verbal bashing real fast.

I've decided that those Tarzan movies should be shown on TV all month in February.

All those control freak government wackos will tell you that drugs are addictive. I bet not one of those dingbats has ever played a video game. You wanna talk about some addictive shit! Man! One game and you are hooked! Shit's worse than crack! Cheaper too. $40 a game and you got a fix that will last a month or more. And you can trade them in once you are done with them! You can't do that with Coke or Heroin, can you? Nope, those are one use drugs, then you need more. Not video games, those can be turned back in for another one, and you are good for another month or so.

Midgets are the coolest. Someone once said to me, "Everything is cool with midgets." And they were right. My only problem with them is, I don't run into them as much as I'd like. And never in the kinds of places I tend to hang out. You never see a gang of midgets wearing leather jackets and riding Harleys. I'd love to see a midget biker gang. And Amish Midgets, you never see any of those either. I have seen midgets playing basketball, and I really think they should form a league. I'd pay money to see that. The MBA. Yep, I'd watch that sooner than I would the NBA, or even the WNBA. Maybe even give them some of those backpack-jet packs. Could you picture that? Jet Assisted Midget Basketball. "Come on down to the Arena and get your JAMB on!" You don't see midgets wrestling anymore either. That was some cool shit. Biting the referee on the ass, that was some classic stuff. You also never see a midget race car driver. Why not? They can drive cars on the street, why not at the races? And one day, I'm going to find a midget porno movie. I'd love to see that. Especially if one of them has a wooden leg! He could take the leg off and use it as a dildo. Hell, maybe it would even look like a dildo.

I wonder what Pauli Shore is doing these days. I actually liked his movies. Very campy, and all based on his stereotypical role, but still funny. Someone compared that dork from the Dell commercials to him, and I had to reply with, "No, the Dell Dork is not entertaining at all. He is annoying." Some argue that Pauli Shore is stupid and annoying, and I can see their point in that, but at least Pauli isn't trying to sell me a piece of junk computer. He's trying to entertain us. And succeeds because he's stupid and annoying. I just wish he'd grow his hair back. He can't do that wild dressing shit with the short hair, he looks gay. With the long hair, he just looks weird. And in my book, weird is good.

Harrison Ford could play a better nigger than Stallone could play a decent hero.

Ok, Sept. 11, 2K2 has come and gone, and there wasn't a fucking thing on TV except the damned memorial shit. Every fucking channel! And on the Spanish Channel(which really pisses me off, because the English channels can be switched to Spanish language for the spicks who can't speak English, but the Spanish channel can't be switched for Americans who refuse to learn Spanish! How right is that shit?!) Anyway, on there, they were showing the shit from the Pentagon, and called it..."El Pentagono"...and I thought to myself, this sounds like a Spick Superhero. "Chill out, man, El Pentagono is here to protect you, homes!" Of course, there aren't any Spick superheroes. Jalapeno Man just doesn't work, and neither does Captain Wetback.

Something I'd like to do at a drive up window one day; when they ask if I would like anything else, tell them that I'd like a new commercial with my order, because the last one sucked.

You know how they are doing all these re-makes, and turning old series into movies? I wonder when they will do a "Greatest American Hero" movie. I'd like to see that, especially if William Katt stars in it, maybe he could hand the alien suit off to someone else.

"What a valiant effort!" I'm sure you've heard that term, know what it means? It means "Nice try, but you still fucked up!"

Here's something we'll never see at the local Arena, the "Bring your own nigger tractor pull."

A new service I wouldn't mind getting started, Lawn Mowing for Beer. All you'd have to do is set a cold beer on your front porch to signify your lawn needs cutting, and once the person starts mowing it, you bring them a cold beer every 20 minutes until the lawn is done. I know several people who would like this job!

I wonder if they make "Binkie Butt Plugs", for potential gays who just aren't sure if they are up to a full sized dildo.

Something I'd like to experience, just to be able to say I had the experience, a blowjob on Feb. 29th.

I saw something that flipped me out...a woman talking on a cell phone at a bus stop. Now, how the fuck can you afford a damned cell phone, and not a fucking car? I know people who have racked up over $700 in one month on a cell phone! How can you afford that and not a $300 a month car payment?!

I wonder if all those chicks getting their clits pierced tie their tampon strings on them? It would keep them from going anywhere now wouldn't it?

I also have to wonder, if somewhere in the world, if there isn't a men only resort called "Cape Fart"?

Schindler was an asshole.

It's a real shame the Nielson Rating System doesn't work like Survivor, that way all the shows would be putting on their best shit so viewers won't vote them off the air.

The Big Bad Wolf, the one from the 3 little pigs story, shoulda used an airplane on the 3rd pigs house. Imagine that, "Fuck that huffin' and puffin' bullshit, RAM A PLANE INTO THAT FUCKERS BRICK HOUSE!"

Why do they call it "Human Resources"? I never see an "Animal Resources", nor do I ever see "Technological Resources", like humans are the only ones that count. I remember when they used to call it "Personnel"...made more sense to me. And since when are humans a resource? Oil is a resource. Humans are a virus on the face of the Earth.

There is nothing more disgusting, or scary, than a dick that is oozing green slime from it. Except a pussy that tastes like year-old sewage.

I'm going to have to sue Geico, that insurance company. They've ruined a good song for me with their latest commercial. Have you seen it? It's the one with "I wanna hold you 'til I die..." and the fat ugly chick doing the "lovers field dance" with the Gecko. I used to like that song, but now when I hear it, I just think of that stupid commercial. And how would a woman make love to a gecko anyway? Shove it in her pussy with only the head sticking out so he can breathe? And smack him on the head to make him wiggle? How does that work?

Two of the biggest things that's fucked up with this world; Beer doesn't multiply in the fridge, and coffee cups don't refill themselves!

Wow, now we are going to attack Iraq again. Junior has to finish up Daddy's work. And people are debating as to whether this is a good idea or not. Personally, I think we shoulda taken the prick out last time. But since we didn't, leave him there. He's had 10 years to build up any weapons he'd want to. I can see a fiasco in the making. The biggest thing I have against military actions, is that the leaders never go into battle. Well, Patton did, but we'll never see another genius like that again. Those that decide to take the action, just sit back on their fat asses and watch the shit on CNN. They never actually get involved, the pussies!

I found out today(09/17/2K2) that it is perfectly legal in the state of MD to threaten to kill someone. As long as you don't actually, do it, or touch them, you can get in their face and tell them you are going to rip their guts out and stomp on them(or anything else you might choose to tell them) and it's no longer a crime. This information is going to come in REALLY useful! However, it is NOT legal to yell out your window(or through an amplifier like I have in my truck) and tell someone that a light is green. This is not bullshit, I had an incident today, I won't go into the details, but I was told this by a Baltimore County cop!

I thought I'd seen it all, but apparently I underestimated the publics gullibility. The latest thing is designer clothes is "waterproof khakis". I know you've seen the commercials, guys spills beer, wine, whatever, down the front of his pants, and the shit just beads up and runs right off. Kinda like they fused the fabric with Rain-X. Now, my first thought is, what if you piss yourself? Ok, so you don't end up with a stain on your pants, where does it go? Right into your shoes my friend. At least those other fabrics will absorb some of it(if not all of it), and you don't end up with squishy feet. And pants are easier to change than your shoes, some people only have one pair of shoes. And now they can be loaded with piss if the line for the potty is too long. What a concept!

The "Anna Nicole Smith Show" is going to go down faster than the XFL!

I saw something you just don't see every day, a biker, on a Harley, with a cell phone on his hip, and sporting a rat tail. For those of you born IN the 80's, a rat tail is a "clean cut" hair style, with one long section of hair trailing down from the upper neck region, and it really does look like a rats tail...hence the name. I haven't seen anyone wearing one of these in well over 10 years. This sight was just one more piece of evidence that the world has already gone to hell.

I've figured out, just by observing people, that I have a legitimate handicap: I'm retardedly challenged. Now all I have to do is get one of those handicap plates for my truck.

People who spay or neuter their pets, and then have kids are hypocrites.

The latest thing at Super Fresh(for those out of the loop, the old A&P stores became a subsidiary of the A&P company and renamed the stores Super Fresh), is these shopping carts with a plastic car built into the front, so you can strap your kids in and let them pretend they are driving around the store. Now, tell me, is this supposed to be teaching them that it's ok to drive IN a supermarket? And who's idea was it to put the HORNS in these fuckers?! Oh, this is great for parents, but annoying as shit for the employees, as well as other patrons. And how long will it be before some teenager runs his car(or more likely a stolen car) into one of these stores and run people down in the produce department screaming "IT'S MORE FUN THAN I REMEMBER AS A KID!!!!"

I saw some really fat people at Wal-Mart the other day, and I don't mean just plain fat, I mean F-A-T!!! They make obese people look anorexic! And then I got to thinking, they can't have any kids, there is just no way these people can have sex! It is physically impossible. The only possible way, without medical intervention, that these two could possibly conceive a child, is if the guy jacks off into his hand, then smears it on her pussy, assuming he can find it!

I saw a funny ad recently in the help wanteds, an "upscale gentlemen's club" (read: Strip Bar for the wealthy) was looking for a "Security Attendant". What the fuck is a "Security Attendant"?! Almost sounds like someone they'd keep on watch in the bathroom to make sure no one uses more than 3 pieces of toilet paper! I checked out their website(which I won't give you), and saw that the entire staff wears pleated-front tuxedo shirts and bow ties. Now, bear with me a second, but just how intimidating could that be? "Pardon me sir, you attempted to touch the nudity professional in an inappropriate manner, I'm afraid I'm going to have to ask you to exit the establishment." Oh yeah, I'd run in fear of this guy! My response to that line would have to be something like "Indeed, I not only attempted to touch her, I did. And she liked it. Just like your wife did this morning. Now get the fuck out of my face, Barney, before I shove that tie up your gay ass!"

Oh joy, the African American festival is this weekend, and all over the news. And it's being held in, guess where? A predominantly WHITE section of town! What the fuck?! Now, I don't begrudge ANYONE of having their ethnic festivals, but lets be fair about this. Also running this weekend are the Korean festival, and the Irish festival(and this one sounds like my kind of shindig! A bunch of drunken red-heads!) But nowhere on the news was anything about the Korean or Irish fests. Why not? Because it's not specifically for blacks or Jews, that's why. And that pisses me off. And since it IS an African festival, I wonder if anyone has an "Apartheid" tent there. I doubt it, since that is like, really part of African culture, and all they really want to celebrate is being black.

If, at this point, I have not offended you, don't worry, you're on my list somewhere, and I'll be getting around to it eventually.

America has no future, it is a country full of lunatics being led by idiots.

Aside from Germany, there are several countries I really want to go to. Scotland, Ireland, Britain, Sweden, Iceland, Italy, Greece(although, I'll have my asshole locked in steel briefs for that trip!) and Australia. I like Aussies, they never fuck with anybody. When was the last time they were in a war? All Aussies ever do is get drunk and fuck kangaroos. They are too busy having fun to fuck with people.

I love this story, I saw it on the news...a woman led her 4 year old daughter out of a store, put her in the car, and beat the shit out of her. But that's not the funny part, I'm getting to that, the funny part is this.... her last name...is "Toogood". They caught this on the security camera, and put it on the news. I laughed my ass off when they told me her name. Apparently, she wasn't toogood to commit child abuse.

Another story in the news lately, is a woman who apparently committed suicide by dumping gasoline in and on her vehicle, and then setting it on fire, with her in it. Went from SUV to BBQ. I just have to wonder, was the SUV a BLAZER?! Would be appropriate now wouldn't it!

Where my fiancé works, she is required to wear a uniform. No big deal here, but it does make employees easy to spot. She was standing outside of the store one day, the store has a huge sign you can read from 3 blocks away, and someone, who was NOT under the influence of anything, actually walked up and asked her "What store is this?" She has also fallen victim to the "Do you work here?" line. And the first thought she had was "No, I'm richer than you can imagine and just get my kicks out of dressing up like employees at stores."

In fact, Koreans, Chinese, Japanese, Thais, Vietnamese, all of those slanty eyed fuckers, do not look alike. Just because they have the same skin tone, does not mean they all look alike. That would be like assuming that (REAL)Bikers, Yuppies, Geeks, Nerds, Dorks, Brits, French and Germans all look the same. They don't. I can point out the differences: Chinese have fat flat faces, Japs are sneaky looking, Koreans have flat faces, but are much more gaunt looking than the Chinese. I don't really see enough Thais and Vietnamese to be able to peg them on sight.

And a note to all you Harley riding yuppie scumbags, you are NOT bikers! I don't care if you are in a "club" or not! Real bikers have tattoos, Harleys(or custom built Choppers), and hate wearing helmets. Real bikers also do not snort cocaine in their plush uptown condo, while their ladies are out on the veranda. No, real bikers do all kinds of crazy shit, and they do them with their "Mamma's" raising hell with them!

The Russian leaders name is Putin(pronounced POOTIN)...I don't know about you, but that sounds like what they call a woman letting out a string of farts. We all know that women don't actually fart, they "poot", well, at least most women, the good ones will fart, and be proud of it. I've got a good one! She'll rip one and claim credit for it. No blaming the dog/cat/weasel for her. Well, sometimes she'll blame me, but only when we are out in public.

I'm not gay, but I do have to admit that I can see some men as good looking. It doesn't mean I want to fuck them, it just means that I can see their attractiveness.

Mel Gibson is a hottie. If I was gay, and he was gay, I'd fuck him. But I'm not, and neither is he.

Fact: Any teenage boy who claims he doesn't masturbate is a liar.

Get ready for a good laugh, I got laid off from the Florist job, so I'm rather free to talk about them any way I want. The head designer, is something I never thought I'd run across...a 31 year old virgin. Can you imagine? And up until recently, hadn't even had a REAL kiss. Talk about a prude, and the pent up sexual frustration she has to endure. I know that women don't really desire sex as much as men do, but come on! She's never seen a penis in real life, and I bet she's never had an orgasm. Now I know that guys are thinking, "Holy shit! A virgin! I want her!" Trust me on this, she isn't the best looking thing walking around, although I have seen worse. Funny thing is, the worse ones can still get laid. Doesn't say much for the men out there. Who the hell would want to teach a 31 year old about sex? Besides, after conversing with her, you'd realize that about the only thing she'd ever try is straight up, missionary position, don't put your mouth on that, and I won't suck anything that doesn't have a straw in it. And she won't let you do it until after the wedding.

Good time to find out you aren't compatible in the bedroom.

Here are the names of some songs I'd like to write someday: "Eat My Cum You Nappy Haired Nigger", "Holy Shit! She Ain't A She!", "Oh Shit...She's Fucking A Spick", "You Border Crossing Wetback", "Mexican Target Practice", "Run You Fucking Nigger", "My Beer Bitch Is A Kike", "Tribute To Honkeys", "She's A Cow...Boy", "Masturbation At Midnight", "Die You Draft Dodging Hippy", "I Hate Fucking Kids(They Scream Too Much)", "Chester Clause", "Bible Thumping Maniacs", "My Five Year Old Smokes", "You're Next Motherfucker", "Smoking Grass And Fucking Your Wife", and "Shove An Egg Timer Up Your Ass".

A new ice cream flavor I saw in the store recently: Banana Boogie. Ok, this must be for the nerds in the populous. I for one, can't see myself eating anything with the name "Boogie" in it. And for you nerds out there, don't tell me to "try it, I might like it", because I refuse to eat my own nasal mucus.

I spotted something at FedEx the other day, a package from a company called "Vegetarian Resource Group"...and I got to thinking, is that a bullshit euphemism for "Produce Stand"? Or are there really people out there who need a company to tell them where you can find produce stands?

Something I've never seen in a porn movie: A flat chested bulldyke with a bald head and a strap-on giving it to scantily clad Norwegian transvestite, while a midget in a sailor suit masturbates in the background.

I'm sure you've seen the anti-drug commercials that starts off with people fading in and out saying shit like "I helped kill a judge." "I helped kill a policeman's family" and that kinda shit...finishes up with "If you do drugs, you help terrorists." My response to you people is: No, if you heat your home with oil, or drive a vehicle that runs on gas, YOU support terrorism! Trust me on this one, most people who do drugs, spend less on them a week than they do on gasoline. Don't hand me that "you help crime" bullshit, judges and lawyers who get the murderers and rapists off are the ones who help crime.

Something I like to do, is when I get right behind a funeral procession, I turn my flashers on, just like they do. I figure, they don't know, and even if they did, what could they do about it. Plus, I get the benefit of running red lights.

Creed is the Stryper of the new millennium, and they suck just as hard.

I remember when you couldn't lose a remote control, because it had a wire going from the control to the unit it was controlling. Of course, Rose and I both remember when we were kids, WE were the remote controls.

Working at FedEx, I noticed something really stupid over there, well, one of many stupid things, but this one made me shake my head. When employees, and "Independent Contractors"(read: delivery drivers) enter or leave the facility, we are gone over with a metal detector, and sometimes patted down. No big deal really, but my question is, when the drivers are on their shift, they aren't searched as they leave with a truck load of packages, only when they are going off their shift. Now, what is to stop them from stealing something out on the road, why the fuck would they be dumb enough to wait until they got back to the terminal? I know they, as well as us package handlers, could be tempted, and we are run through the standard background checks, but gimme a fucking break!

The news has become a fucking joke in Baltimore. We've got a sniper running loose in the DC and Virginia area, and every fucking time this dingbat shoots someone, the Baltimore news cuts into any show that's on, and gives us absolutely NO information. Then they rehash the shit for 3-4 hours, still calling it "Breaking News". It was breaking news when it started, and we got all the new information within the first 30 seconds, then get it repeated for hours on end. I hope that sniper starts nailing the fucking news crews!

Speaking of the "Beltway Sniper" as he or she has been dubbed,(and don't think it can't be a woman, although the shit has been going on for two weeks at this point, don't think PMS, think MENOPAUSE! Or maybe even a woman who has been abused and finally snapped, don't think it's a man just because this person is a crack shot and is smart enough to evade police. I would have said that it would take a woman to outsmart them, but this is the Maryland, DC, and Virginia police we are talking about here.) Anyway, it's now been brought out that the military will be flying a spy plane over the area now...Ok, I can see the logic of actually doing this, but telling everyone about it?! And the police are being very, ummm, shall we say, secretive? Well, until I can come up with a better way to describe it, it will have to do. But I digress. The police are not releasing much in the way of information, they don't want to sniper to know what they know. BUT! They want the publics help in locating the sniper. So we are looking for a white box-truck with "UNKNOWN WORDS" written on the side. Ok, they are only three or four of those in the Baltimore/Washington/Virginia area...should be easy to spot. No problem. Just a side note, anyone who didn't see that dripping with sarcasm needs to be shot immediately, so please, do us all a public service and take care of this matter.

We were watching the 2nd annual running of the Baltimore Marathon this morning. Boy did we have some comments about this stupidity. Anyone who gets out of bed at 5:30 am, to run 26 miles starting at 8:00 am, must be out of their mind. The winner was some black guy from Kenya, and we wondered if he trained for this race by running from the police, or white supremacist? I figure the latter, since he wasn't carrying a DVD player or a TV set across the finish line. Something else we saw, was when the first woman(A Russian named Kornakova, a name I immediately thought sounded like a Star Wars character) crossed the finish line, they came up and wrapped her in this tinfoil looking blanket. I said, "Wrap her up in foil and shove her in the oven." Rose replied with, "No need to baste her." I replied to that with, "Finally, a self basting runner." I bet there are some Jewish readers taking serious offense to this one. Something else, in case any of you are wondering why I think this is stupid, remember, the "Beltway Sniper" was still on the loose, talk about "Targets On Parade"!!! That's one reason. Another is that whole 5:30 am thing...I'd be hard pressed to get up that early if the house was on fire.

Oh boy, something new...Extreme Variety. A new TV show or special, some such shit. From the commercial I just saw, it seems like something that is the Gong Show of the 21st century. And no, this is NOT a good thing!

Something else about this Marathon, was the commentary. Apparently the reporters left their brains at home. "This is a hilly race on this hilly day." What the fuck is a hilly day?! Live TV can be entertaining, but you have to pay attention to catch all the fuckups.

I realized something earlier, if all we had to do was piss, the sit-down toilet would not have been invented until the late 20th century. Toilets were invented by men, and lets face it, men can piss standing up. And you know how men are, especially way back when. They didn't care about women, or their problems. They considered them property. Kinda like niggers. And if this doesn't tell you something; the niggers could be bought and sold, the women couldn't. Tells you about how much they were valued, nothing. Although, if you think about it, wives couldn't be sold, but daughters could. Where do you think the concept of the "Dowry" came from? And if you don't know what a dowry is, look it up and learn something. That's also where the concept of "Giving the Bride Away" came from, the parents approved of the marriage, but the grooms parents didn't have a dowry. So they just gave her away.

Were you aware that the United Nations has an "Adopt a Minefield" program? I'm not making this up! I want one! I just wonder if I can move it from where it is, to over here where I want it. I want it placed at several busy intersections in and around Baltimore. Bet they won't let me do that. Maybe I could at least put it in my back yard. Heh, you'll obey that "No Trespassing" sign next time won't you, Shorty?

Okay, they caught the snipers, there actually were two of them, and what a crew. If you don't think liberals are helping to ruin this country, think about this: The main picture that was flashed on the news, was of the two men sitting in a living room, smiling like hell. Making them look like happy-joy-joy people. The original picture of the older guy that they originally flashed up, was a military picture, and he looked like a psycho. That picture got lost real fast when they found the smiley picture.

Speaking of the snipers, did you hear that they are a Father-Stepson duo? I like this. This is family bonding! "Well son, how would you like to go hunting this week?" "Gee Dad, sounds like fun!" "Good, I have several places picked out, where would you like to go? Micheals? Home Depot? The Steakhouse?" "Well, Dad, we hit the Micheals last week, how about the Home Depot?" "Excellent choice. You drive, and I'll take the trunk." The sad part is, that's more "family bonding" than many fathers are willing to commit to.

I really feel for the decent people of Montgomery County, if there are any. Having someone like "Chief Moose" in charge of the police department makes me want to buy body armour. This guy couldn't catch a cold, for Christ's sake! And what a wonderful speaker he is. I just know that fucker is going to get elected Governor. I can see it coming. And I can hear the State of the State address... "The state of the State, is appropriate. Thank you."

People where I work, they love me. Co-workers actually do, but management and security consider me a major pain in the ass. I love fucking with people who think they are better than me. Actually, the security people are pretty cool, they are just working people like us. I do fuck with them though, but they are really good natured about it. Management hates me for it. And the best part is, there isn't anything they can do about it. I don't have or need a union to back me up, my work ethic speaks for itself. They'd never be able to find someone who works like I do. I bust my ass, and their balls, all at the same time. I'm a multi-tasking sumbitch. When I start working somewhere, I establish just how good I am. I tell them straight out, then back it up by doing it. Then I start letting them know that I am a rotten fucker, as well as one of the smartest bastards they are ever going to meet.

I really like Anne Robinson. She's a bitch with attitude. I love women like that, hell, I'm engaged to one! The shame is, that there are lots of men out there who need a woman like this. The abusive bastards top the list. Those nits who use the line "I own you, you are my property." That kinda shit. They need one of those bitches to straighten them up. Just remember asshole, you gotta sleep sometime. Just ask John Wayne Bobbit.

I never trust a skinny cook. Except for very few, most good cooks are fat. And it makes sense, they love to eat, and they want good food. Of course, I don't eat in shabby looking diners, so the fat-slob cook thing is not something I have to deal with. First thing I do when I sit down, is ask to see the cook. If he or she isn't fat, I walk out.

Some things that have changed: "A Suspect" has become "A Person of Interest.", an "Interrogation" became "Questioning", but recently moved onto an "Interview". Next time I get pulled over, I'm going to make sure to say this to the cop, "Good day Protector of the City(or county, whichever is appropriate), I feel the compulsion to inform you that I am an interesting person, however not a person of interest, and there is no need for an extended detention for a thorough interview at your protective community center."

This just in: Biggs California is going to change it's name to "Got Milk". I am watching this on the news as I type this. What the fuck?! They are actually putting this up for a vote, and if it goes through, not only does the name of the town change, but they get a big cash infusion from some corporation or organization. I knew it would happen, it started with naming arenas, then stadiums, and now it's coming to a town near you. I can see where this is going; "K-Y Kentucky", "Tampax Texas", "Trojan Alaska", "Frosted Flakes Washington", "Fruit Loops DC", "Dildo Dakota", "Vibrator Vermont", "Microsoft Washington", "Little Sister West Virginia".

Something that just struck me, some of you have read a lot of this shit, and on the stuff like tying tampon strings to clit rings, some of you are actually thinking about doing it. Admit it, way in the back of your head, you're actually thinking this is a good idea, and something to try. Speaking of piercings and good ideas, how come you never see anyone getting a ring in their sphincter? Go down to your local shop and ask about that one. "I want my asshole pierced." Do it, and then look at the face of the clerk with all seriousness, and try to not bust out laughing at their reaction.

I saw an ad recently on the side of a vehicle, "Professional Residential Lawn Maintenance Service Technicians." How in the purple fuck did that come about?! When I was a kid, we cut lawns for a buck, now this asshole with a title longer than my dick comes along and wants $50!

Working at FedEx is like bowling with square balls.

Idiots are so entertaining. I saw a guy standing in the middle of the street yammering on a cell phone. Just pacing back and forth, staring at the ground and running his mouth. I'm thinking to myself, "All I need to make this situation better is for a speeder to come flying by and not see this retard until it's too late." Shame it didn't happen.

I scared the fuck out of a kid one time, he needed it though. He crossed the street without looking. Just walked right out in front of me. Now, I was sitting at a red light, and this kid started crossing. I woke his ass up when I put the truck in neutral, kept my foot on the brake, but floored the gas pedal at the same time. The engine roared, and this kid shit himself. I laughed like hell.

Now that the Snipers have been caught, I want to get myself one of those white box trucks that they were hunting for(for those who haven't heard, they were caught in a blue or purple colored Chevy Caprice, which is really hard to distinguish from a white box truck), but I want to get a truck like that, and paint "UNKNOWN WORDS" down the side of it(in other words, make it look like the picture they were showing on the non-news). Once the paint is dry, I'm going driving around town to see what happens.

If it wasn't for Morton Downey Jr, Jerry Springer wouldn't have a job. Downey did it first, better, and with an attitude.

There are actually people out there who dress their dogs up to look like them! Same coats, sweaters, hats, all that shit! What the fuck is up with that?! "Look Penelope, Fido looks just like me! Isn't that special?!"

Do you really think your dog gives a fuck? I think the dog is more likely to be embarrassed by this shit. Unless he/she can claim to the other dogs that the human wants to be like him/her. And what the hell is next? Canine make-overs? Putting the same color nail polish on the Poodle as what you are wearing? Get a life you morons!

As everyone knows, the Prez's nickname is "W". Just one letter...kinda like "Q" from Star Trek...only the reverse. "Q" was omnipotent, intelligent beyond imagining... "W" BELIEVES he's omnipotent, but is really stupid beyond belief. I would have said "Thinks" there, but everyone knows he doesn't. The funny thing is, "W" is about as long of a nickname as his pathetic brain could handle.

I live with my Grandmother, there is a long story there, but I am not a mooch. I'm not your typical "guy living with his parents." She doesn't have anyone else, and couldn't keep the house if I wasn't here. I admit, I do get off a little easy on the rent thing, but still, I'm here for whatever she needs. Anyway, there was a time when I had moved out, to be on my own. Kinda was, kinda wasn't. A then friend of mine and I rented an apartment together. It was your typical bachelor pad, lots of parties, drinking, loud music, messy as hell(at least until the parties, then we'd clean up.) Anyone who has lived in an apartment knows, when someone is right over top of you, you can hear them walking around up there. You deal with it. That wasn't a problem, but what was a problem was when those assholes up there started dropping shit(sounded like a 15 lb bowling ball) on the floor, at 2:00 am every morning, in every room. Like fucking clockwork. That got old real quick. We tried beating on the ceiling, cranking the stereo, nothing worked. Hell, we even tried talking to them about it. My room mate's Grandmother worked with the police department, and had a police scanner. A plan began to form. We ironed out the details, sent out the invitations(yeah right, we called about 50 people, including everyone in the building except the assholes upstairs.) Got us a keg of beer, and we were ready. I have to backtrack a little bit at this point. My room mate and I were both chess players(something that requires lots of brains to play, you just wouldn't understand), and we planned this when there was an amateur chess tournament coming up. We laid out the ground rules when everyone showed up, drink as much as you want, but do not sit your cup down anywhere. Make as much noise as you want, but don't touch the chessboard on the coffee table. In other words, leave no signs of a party, anywhere! If you are wondering as to the why's of this...keep reading, you'll find out soon enough. We set the chessboard up with a few moves already made, had a timer set on the one side of the board(this is how it is done at chess tournaments, and we were allegedly practicing for the one coming up), and a log book with the moves made at each players right. We put someone in the apartment across the hall, the far bedroom with the police scanner and adequate beer. The scene was set up, and everyone informed of the rules. The party started. We kicked the stereo up to 7, and began raising hell. About a half hour had gone by, when the "Ears"(code word for who was set up with the radio) came over and informed us that the cops had been called. We shut the stereo off, and everyone moved into the apartment across the hall. The lights over there were turned off, Jim sat on one side of the board, I on the other, and a designated driver took the "referee's" position. We waited. Sure enough, here came the knock on the door. The "Referee" answered the door, while my room mate and I stared at the chessboard, looking like we are concentrating. The "referee" opened the door far enough so the cop could look in and see that no party was going on, just a couple of guys playing chess. The cop explained that he had gotten a call about a wild loud party here, so the "referee" left the door open, but motioned for the cop to keep his voice down, then began to explain about the people upstairs and the upcoming chess tournament, and how they had known about it, and since there was some "bad blood" that they were doing everything they could to disrupt the practice. The cop admitted that he hadn't been sure about the address, and even had to radio back the station to verify the address. It was all my room mate and I could do to keep a straight face. The cop finished off with "Well, I can see there is nothing going on here, but since we did get a call, I have to tell you to keep it down. Sorry about disturbing you." And he left. About five minutes after he left, we sent out troops to scan the area to make sure he wasn't waiting around, changed "Ears", turned the stereo up to 8, moved the chess pieces up a few moves, and commenced the party again. About 45 minutes later, the "Ears" came over and told us that another call had gone out. Again, we shuffled everyone over to the other apartment and settled down to wait. The knock on the door came, and the "referee" opened the door just like the first time, only it was a different cop(we thought this was great, at this point there were two cops to back up our story about no party), he was also quite polite and apologetic about having to disturb us. The "referee" gave him the same story he gave the first cop. The cop gave us the obligatory "keep it quiet" and left. We sent the troops out again, and since the cop didn't wait around, everyone came back and we turned the stereo up to 9. Can you see a pattern here? Within a half hour(it was about 12:30 at this point, and we were just getting settled into the party), the "ears" came over and told us the third call had gone out. Again, we shut everything down, and everyone went to the other apartment. When the "referee" opened the door, it was the same cop that had shown up the first time. He didn't seem to be in a good mood anymore. He told us that something was going on, and they were getting tired of it. At this point, the idiot upstairs decided to get involved personally, since he knew what was going on. He came stomping down the steps, and was obviously intoxicated. He started screaming at the cop(bad move number one), shouting about how everyone had moved into the other apartment(at this revelation, we completely and totally failed to panic). Apparently the guy who rented the apartment across the hall had been paying attention to what was going on out in the hall. He hustled everyone into the two bedrooms, and the kitchen(anywhere that wasn't in sight of the door), then took off all his clothes, knowing what was about to happen. The idiot upstairs(and no, I'm not trying to protect him, I just don't remember his name), demanded of the cop(bad move number two), to go into the apartment and see for himself. I give the cop credit, he was more than patient with an obvious drunk swearing and making demands of him. Finally, my room mate and I got up from the table, and told the cop, "Make him happy, and prove for yourself that nothing is going on here, knock on the door." The cop knocked on the door, and after a minute the guy across the hall opened the door, the tuft of hair on his head was in disarray, he stood there naked, and looking half asleep. "Whah? Oh, hi officer." He then scratched his ample belly. I don't think the cop was any too happy at this sight. I taunted the idiot upstairs by laughing silently at him(of course, the cops back was to me, I'm not stupid!) Mr. Moron decided to take the opportunity to try and jump past the cop, who grabs him, and pushes him back up the steps, telling him that if he makes another move like that, he's going to jail tonight. The cop asks the guy across the hall about any noise, parties, or anything we might have been doing to cause a disturbance. The guy across the hall explained to the cop, rather slurredly(we was supposed to be half asleep, you know) that no, we had been quiet all night, and were probably practicing for that upcoming chess tournament. When he said this, the moron went off. He demanded that the cop enter the apartment and search it(bad move number three!) The cop apologized to the guy across the hall for disturbing him, then apologized to us for the disturbance, and shuffled the moron up the steps. The guy was screaming and yelling at the cop(bad move number FOUR!) The cop finally told him that "If you call us again tonight, YOU are going to jail where you can settle down. Now leave these people alone!" The guy across the hall closed the door, we went back in our apartment, and started laughing like hell! Like they say in those infomercials, "But wait, there's MORE!" The guy stomped back to his apartment and slammed the door. The cop left, but this time hung around outside for about 10 minutes before leaving(I guess he was on the radio with the precinct). We changed "ears" again(it was a rotating shift), moved the pieces again, and fired up the party, this time with the stereo on 10. This time, it didn't even take 15 minutes for the call to go out. We shut the party down again, and waited...and waited...and waited...45 minutes later, the cops had still not shown up. I guess they were tired of running out here, or maybe they had something better to do. In any case, we figured it was safe and fired the party back up, since the stereo was already on 10, I hit the "LOUD" button(which kicked it up even higher). They tried calling again, and we knew the calls had gone out, but the cops had called back to dispatch to ignore those calls, they were bogus. The party finally broke up about 8:00am the next morning. You'd think they'd have learned their lesson about fucking with us...

Needless to say, they hadn't. My room mate and I decided to lay low for about a month. We figured if the cops kept getting involved, eventually they'd figure out that we were setting them up. It was a sunny Sunday afternoon, and the asshole upstairs was particularly noisy. Something was up, we both knew it. Another plan formed in our heads. I found a loose board(actually, it wasn't loose, but it had a wedge missing next to the wall at one end.) Armed with hammer, I decided to find out what affect this discovery had on the asshole. I banged it a few times, then heard "STOMP, STOMP, STOMP, STOMP, *WHAM*(the door slamming) STOMP, STOMP, STOMP..." Down the steps he was coming. He pounded on our door(it was unlocked, as it always was when we were home during the day, it was our custom that if we were available, the door was unlocked and those who knew it could just walk in.) And shouted through the door to "Keep the fucking noise down or I'll come in there and fuck you up!" We yelled back(without locking the door) "Go back upstairs you dickhead! I need to fix this loose board!" He pounded on the door some more, and threatened to kill us if the noise didn't stop. Then he stomped back upstairs and slammed his door. I guess it's fine for him to make all the noise he wants, but we can't make a sound. Anyway, we got an idea. I opened our door, the closed it(but not enough for the latch to engage), and propped a Pepsi bottle(they were made of glass back then) up against it, to hold it closed(or at least appear closed). My room mate picked up the phone(it was a cordless) and held it behind his back. I tucked my survival knife into the back of my pants, and went to work on the board again. "STOMP, STOMP, STOMP, STOMP, *WHAM* STOMP, STOMP, STOMP..." Here he came again... and when he hit our door, it flew open, the Pepsi bottle sailed under a chair(what a luck shot!) Then he made a huge mistake...he stepped into our apartment. I told him to stay right where he was, my room mate pulled out the phone, and called 911. He said, right in front of the idiot, "I'd like to report a breaking and entering in progress." The cops showed up in quick order, and the moron just stood there. We told the cop what happened(about the loose board, the threats of violence against us, and then that he just came in, we assumed to follow through.) The cop put the cuffs on him. Then he informed us that he had brought the guy home instead of locking him up for a drunk and disorderly call at a local 7-11. As the cop was taking him out, his mother came flying out of her apartment(talk about worse than living with your parents, living with your parents in a 2 bedroom apartment!) She bitched at the cop about how he "Can't take my baby to jail!" She seemed quite adamant about the subject, until the cop informed her that there was room in the car for her too. She then tossed some insults down to us, and made a threat to us about getting us back for this. I guess the apple really doesn't fall far from the tree.

There is one more little story about those days I want to relate to you, and just like the stuff above, is all true. I think it's rather obvious that I enjoy fucking with peoples heads. Religious Fanatics are among the top on that list. Jehovah's Witnesses are particularly fun to fuck with. One bright and cheery Sunday morning, they came knocking. Across the hall is apartment A, my room mate and I in apartment B. The guy across the hall and his wife are both Pagans, as am I, and my room mate follows old Indian ways(he is part Cherokee). The guy across the hall also liked to debate with nuts. Like all apartments, the walls were paper thin, and you could hear what is going on in the hall. I watched as these two nutballs were talking with the guy in A. I got an idea, and quickly did a set up. My room mate helped me set up a shitload of black candles, I put on a black cloak-looking robe, and waited for the knock. When it finally came, my room mate was back in his bedroom with the door closed. I had also pulled out my hardcover-leather-bound copy of the "Hitchhiker's Guide to the Galaxy", opened the book to a page, and made sure the cover couldn't be seen. When the knock on the door came, I called out in a deep, almost satanic voice, "You may enter." They opened the door and stepped in, and stopped dead in their tracks. They saw the candles, the leather-bound book, and me in a black cloak(at least it looked like one), I bid them to enter and sit down. They stepped in a little more, but did not sit down. They also left the door open, which I assume was to provide a quick escape. I looked down at the book, and "read" to them: "Yay, and the land shall be covered in darkness, his minions in the guise of believers in Jehovah, shall walk forth and bring to him the souls of those who are weak of mind. Those who claim to be his Witness', shall one day know his name, Diabolese, The Lord of Darkness." I was just getting ready to hit them with more, when they beat a hasty retreat. The funny thing is, I think they had been really shaken up, cuz they went straight to their car without bothering anyone else in the neighborhood.

And people call ME sick! Who in the fuck came up with the idea of using oysters for turkey stuffing? Fuck, if you are going to do that, save the money and just blow your nose into the fucking turkey! Christ people, use some decency! Isn't it bad enough you're celebrating theft, rape and murder on "Thanksgiving"? Do you have to bring salt-water mucus into it?!

I used to be a wrestling fan, it was recently the shit got stupid. For those of you out of the loop, the WWF bought WCW, and that is where it all started. It was cool, with the whole "Invasion" storyline was going good, then that was over, and sometime early in 2K2, Vinny-Mac hired Eric Bischoff, the dickhead responsible for fucking WCW up and running it into the ground. That did it for me. The shit went downhill after that. They ended up having to change their name to WWE(World Wrestling Entertainment), because the World Wildlife Foundation got a wild hare up their ass about the WWF logo. I'm not against wildlife, far from it. I stand up for wildlife over people. But that pissed me off. WWF sounds a lot tougher that WWE. Anyway, I know what a lot of you are thinking, "oh God! Wrestling! EWWWW! Doesn't he know Rasslin is FAKE?!" DUH!! Doesn't everyone?! When the whole "it's fake" shit started, I was annoying the piss out of people, because I knew it was staged. Actually, "fake" isn't really a word I would use. "Staged" is. Look at it for what it is, a production to entertain us. It's a show. When you go to a movie, do you say shit like "WOW! Look at Stallone spraying those blanks at all those guys! They sure do look like they are getting shot up, even though we know they aren't! And those squibs, the timing of them makes it really look like they are being shot! Can you believe the timing of the explosives on that miniature set?! Far out!" Hell no, you don't say shit like that! You say shit like "Holy fucking shit man! Rambo just shot all those Jap bastards right to hell! Then he fucking blew their fucking embassy to shit man! Fuckers deserved it for fucking with Rambo! He killed all those motherfuckers!" So get off my ass when I say shit like "The Undertaker picked up Shawn Michaels and drilled him head first into the mat!" Look at it this way, not one of these wrestlers has a stunt man, they ARE the stuntmen! The shit they do takes skill, and there is risk involved. One wrong move, and someone gets hurt for real. I've seen the shit happen, as most of the shows have been live for the past 5-6 years.

It's really fucking pathetic when the only thing on TV worth watching is the TV Guide channel!

Speaking of TV, it makes me think of the news, which also makes me think of the weather. Where the fuck did the weatherman go? And who is this asshole "Meteorologist"? Where did this dingbat come from? The weatherman used to make decent predictions, now this meteorologist show up, boots the weatherman aside, and he couldn't tell you the weather if he looked out the window!

Baltimore is really fucked up...it's the middle of November, and we have a tornado watch going on right now.

All right, shit is really getting out of hand. How can anyone be so fucking busy, that they need to FLOSS at a fucking red light?! Give me a break! Do that either at home, or in the bathroom at the fast food joint to were just at! If you have to eat in the car, eat and floss before you leave the fucking parking lot! People have too many distractions when they are driving as it is, do we need another one?! Cell phones, laptop PCs, DVD players in the car?! WHAT THE FUCK?! Why don't you just shove a satellite dish up your ass and stay the fuck home! Christ, no wonder we have so many accidents! "Sorry officer, the movie I was watching got to the good part, while I was answering an e-mail from my boss, and I damn near spilled my coffee when that jerk hit his brakes for that red light!"

Notice to all fat and ugly people out there: Please refrain from wearing any, and I do mean ANY, cutsey "pick me up" shirts. I'm talking about the ones that read: "Princess", "Heart Breaker", "Daddy's Little Girl/Princess/etc..", and the nefarious, "I'm the best lay you'll never get." I got news for you, no one with any decency wants to lay you. It's more like something someone should read TO you, not off of you!

I get a lot of material off of the morning news. I saw a piece on a show this morning, and the irony of it struck me as hysterical. Target, the store, has pulled a big fucking ship into a harbor somewhere in New York. Meanwhile, an earlier story mentioned a new threat from the Terrorists, aimed at crippling the economy again, and I'm thinking, how appropriate...a ship with Targets all over it! Like hang a fucking sign out! "Terrorists Strike Here!" Could the timing have been any better for this?

I also get some of my material from the places I work, or have worked. I already mentioned this guy "Twirkle" at FedEx, the one with the Gay-Irklesque lisp. Well, something I've noticed, is that he tends to use the word "Package" quite a bit. Now, I know American slang is difficult to grasp for foreigners, about as difficult as English is for the natives of America(not the Indians, you moron, I'm talking about the honkeys and the niggers who are born here!) Anyway, "Twirkle" likes to use the term "package", I prefer the word "Box". And if you look at our respective sexual preferences, you will see how the slang terminology factors into this. "Box" is a slang term for the female genetalia, "Package" is a slang term for the male genetalia. I prefer women, and I use the term Box. "Twirkle", who I admit closely resembles a gay person, but who's preference I really don't know, prefers to use the term Package. Does this really mean anything? I think so.

Call me a nerd if you want, but I've had a computer in my house for over 20 years. I've forgotten more about computers than most of you point-and-clickers will ever know. Hell, at this point, I've got over 20 computers in my home, have six of them set up, and half of those are on a network. I still use the older systems, they were great in their day. Shit, there is stuff my Amigas can still do that my IBM compatibles can't. And, for those of you who haven't had a computer all that long, any winblows computer is an IBM compatible. It's pretty fucking sad when a ten year old, 25mhz computer can multi-task better than a state of the art 1.8Ghz computer. There is something wrong there, and that prick Gates is responsible for it. The part that really gets me though, is people who say "But windows is all there is." And mean it! Even on outdated hardware, the Amiga's OS can compute circles around windows. There are at least 2 decent OSs out there for the IBM compatibles, Unix, and Linux. They still aren't up to the standards set forth by the Amiga, but at least they are stable! Windows will crash if you look at it the wrong way.

For those of you out there who will add any component, plug-in, update, whatever, that comes across your screen, you get what you deserve when the machine crashes. If you don't know what you are doing with them, then shut it off, and walk the fuck away.

I remember back in the old days of computers, only smart people had them, because you needed a brain to use one. We were ridiculed for it, Digitheads, Nerds, Geeks, Dorks, etc...well, now the morons who teased us have computers, and are constantly fucking them up. Guess who fixes them for you, asswipe? The very same people you used to tease for having them. Don't think we can't, and don't scan your hard drive, just to see all the porn you downloaded because your spouse finally figured out you are a brain-dead shitball, and doesn't want to fuck you anymore.

You know, I remember when you could watch TV at night, and watch the stations sign off. And if you were watching the late movie, and fell asleep, you'd wake up and see the Test Pattern on the screen. Now, you wake up to some asshole trying to sell you something at 4:00 am. Who the fuck wants to watch a 30 minute commercial? I get pissed when the 30 second ones interrupt my shows! Who's idea was this anyway? I take notes on who does those infomercials(euphemism for a half-hour commercial, to make it sound informative), and refuse to ever buy the product.

I am a rotten motherfucker. I'm sure you're smart enough to figure that out by now, then again, maybe not. Another example of how mean I can be, I was working at a restaurant one time, and we had this one cook there(a skinny guy, which should tell you something), but he was an arrogant sumbitch. I hate people who are arrogant and aren't as good as they think. This guy, whose name I can't remember, was the type to piss everyone off, just by being an annoying asshole. And the worst part was that he often wondered why no one liked him. DUH! Anyway, he was also one of the biggest pussies I've ever met. One beer, one sissy beer(like Bud, Coors, etc..), and his ass was wasted. We were in the parking lot after work one night, tossing down a couple of beers, and had a pre-formulated plan. Here's how it unfolded...he came out and started hanging around, so we handed him a beer. After a bit, he went back in to take a whiz, and we put a miniature of vodka into his beer(1/2 hour and only 1/3 of the beer had been consumed). After he came back out, we decided to go driving around. So we head downtown. It wasn't long before he had finished the beer, and passed out cold. We rode down to the "red light" section of town(where the strip bars, adult stores, etc... are all in one place) we carry his passed out carcass into one of the places and shout to the bartender, "This dude is sick, where is your bathroom?!" He pointed and we hauled him in. We stripped him naked, put a derby style hat and a pair of sunglasses on him, and left him in the stall. We snuck out one at a time. He failed to show up for work the next day. When he did report for work, he said next to nothing to us all night(talk about a blessing!)...but we finally cornered him, and asked him where the hell he ran off to that night. He swore up and down we had done him dirty(we had, but no one was going to admit to it!) and gotten him arrested. Trying like hell to keep a straight face and pretend we didn't know what happened(well, we didn't know what happened after we had left him), we told him that: "We were all walking down by the harbor, when all of the sudden you started screaming, running around like a nut, tearing off your clothes, then ran away. We tried to catch you, but after you turned the corner, by the time we got there, you had disappeared. So we picked up your clothes and went driving around looking for you, but didn't see you anywhere." We almost DIED laughing when he told us about being found in the bathroom of the strip club. We really didn't think they'd call the police on him, and we never did find out if he got a fine or anything. We do know he spent the night in jail, but we were unable to learn the final outcome.

All you MADD mothers can piss off, we always had a designated driver. This one guy was on constant medication, and couldn't drink. He was the "designated mobile party babysitter", back when you could still get away with it. Besides, at the time, he was the only one of us with a car. We would get a case or two of beer, and go riding around. We may be drunks, but we are responsible drunks. Party hard people, but party

SMART! Maybe if that was MADDs message, we'd get along better with those people.

Jeffrey Jones, that guy that played the principal in "Ferris Bueller's Day Off", along with some other minor roles I can't think of at the moment, has been put behind bars for molesting a 14 year old boy. Now, my question to this is...When the hell did he get ordained?! Shit, I didn't even know he was a Catholic!

I've decided, that since I am more than a little familiar with the old computers, you know, the ones before they had a mouse....you actually had to type in what you wanted the machine to do...and all this "Retro" shit that's going around, I am now to be referred to as a "Retro-Technologist".

I heard something this morning that made my jaw drop. All the retarded kids are gone. Now we have children who have a condition known as "Pervasive Developmental Delay Disorder." You know what really sucks about this euphemism shit? The fact that before you can call someone the P.C. Version of the insult you had cooking in your mind, they have already beat the fuck out of you because you took too long to say it all!

We had a funny incident today...I ran my girlfriend over to pick up her paycheck, and as we were leaving the parking spot, I turned to go up the aisle and had to stop. I had to stop because some black cunt was backing out of her spot, and made four attempts to do it. I said, "Learn how to drive that fucking car or park it permanently!", to which the love of my life said, "Yeah, ride the bus, you can sit in the front now!" We sat there for a good five minutes while I finished laughing.

Have you ever been to one of those "Monster Truck Rally's"? I haven't. Talk about some stupid shit, watching trucks race over cars...not normal trucks, oh no! But specially designed and built trucks, with tires big enough to raise the Titanic. What the hell? And here's part of my point...most of these events(at least the ones in my area) are held INDOORS! So, you have these huge trucks, with huge engines, spewing out massive amounts of exhaust, INDOORS! Now, what is the main gaseous material in exhaust? Carbon-Dioxide. Now, pay attention, this might go over your head. Especially all you dingbats associated with that "Infect Truth" bullshit. Go to one of these events, and try to smoke a cigarette in the stands. They won't let you, in fact, they might throw you out. Like a fucking cigarette is going to give everyone in the place fucking cancer, but you can trust them on this...that carbon-dioxide laced exhaust is absolutely harmless. A little cigarette will give everyone in the place lung cancer.... but the exhaust won't hurt them a bit. Ok, now, how many of you are still with me on this? Probably not many. It's like at the stadiums...you can smoke out on the concourse, where the food is, and it's fairly closed in...but not out in your seat, where it's wide fucking open. All right, now...about this smoking in the workplace bullshit...I can see few places where I agree with this...I am a smoker(oh my God! He's a smoker! CHILD KILLER!!!), but I have a brain(and anyone who says "how can he have a brain if he's a smoker?" To you, I say, FUCK OFF! My smoking has kept many of you assholes alive!) Anyway, I agree with no smoking around food. But, here's my complaints...there are some places where the smoking won't hurt anyone, and sure as fuck won't BOTHER anyone. Take for example, the Toll Takers. Here you are, stuck in a small space, with only one open window, but what is constantly floating in that window...CAR EXHAUST! A fucking cigarette won't hurt these people any...and it sure as shit won't float into your car. Let them smoke there! And places like FedEx, and probably UPS as well... huge, wide open warehouse like place, where trucks drive in and park. Let them smoke in there! Trust me, it won't bother anyone, except maybe the most extremely sensitive...and they shouldn't be working at a place like that anyhow. Like it isn't bad enough we get chased outside, where in the winter time we can get sick and die from exposure, but that isn't as bad as getting cancer, is it? No, you pricks would rather we get pneumonia and die quick rather than get cancer and drag it out. If my point has gone over your head.... the please put a bullet in it. Your head numbnuts, not my point!

I've been digging around my memory for some older stuff that I did when I was young, because the news has been quite lax in giving me new shit to write about. That's ok, I've got a lot of shit I've done in my life to relate to you. You can easily figure out which is which, as the old shit I did when I was younger will start off with "I remember one time...."...as opposed to "Today....."

Al Gore didn't invent the Internet...as far as I can tell...he didn't even have a modem back in the old BBS(Bulletin Board System) days. I did. You can thank people like me who used computers back then for the Internet...we didn't invent it...but without our support for BBSs, and later networking(such as FidoNet, and a whole lot of others), the internet would not exist.

Last night(hey, a new opening for a paragraph! Holy shit!), I fucked with our supervisor, Nate. He's pretty cool for the management type. I called him over while I was unloading a truck, and said..."Nate, you gotta do me a huge favor man." He asked what, and I said this: "Dude, you gotta talk to the construction people working out on Route 7, give them a kick in the ass to finish that shit up!" Just to explain, they tore up the road, and replaced ONE lane of asphalt. So by the time you cross the road, you need a new suspension in your car! He again, asked me why he should do this. "Nate, you know how bumpy it is out there now, I almost spilled my beer crossing that shit on the way to work tonight!" He shook his head, and busted out laughing. I'm honestly not sure if he thought I was joking or not. I've gotten them so confused about when I am joking, and when I'm not, they really don't know how to take it anymore.

I remember one time, me and some College friends(all with long hair, biker jackets, ripped jeans, concert shirts....you know the fashion of the early '90s) were walking through the mall. We were just hanging out, not looking for any trouble or anything, we weren't the type. We never looked for trouble, we weren't thieves, or anything like that. But, and I'm sure the blacks who read this can relate, we were targets for discrimination. It didn't take long before we spotted the "plain clothes rent-a-cops" following us, watching our every move. We decided to fuck with them. We went through every store in the mall, picking up shit, looking it over, and putting it back. We even got into moving around so as to block their view from time to time when picking shit up. We'd put it back when they weren't looking. They followed us for a few hours, and we finally led them to a pizza place in the mall. We walked in, ordered food and a pair of soda's each. We hadn't even finished ordering when they strolled in and sat down(now that's not obvious...sitting at a table without having ordered anything). We got our food, and sat down the plates, and one soda. Then we walked over to them and put a soda in front of each of them. They looked at us like "what the fuck are you people doing." After staring at us for what seemed like hours, one of them finally asked "What is this for?" I spoke up: "Well, we figure you've got to be thirsty after following us around the mall for the last three hours." Then we sat back down and ate. They all got up and left without touching the sodas we bought them. I'm not sure, but I think we pissed them off.

And here comes Christmas...and all of it's associated stupidity. I suppose I can thank that Sept. 11th shit...it seems to have brought some sanity back to this mayhem. It was just a few years ago, when you would hear those annoying songs before Halloween. At least now the shit is back to starting after Thanksgiving(which should be Thankstaking!). Something that hasn't changed in the last few years, is those fucking hard up stores opening at Five-Fucking-Thirty!!! I admit, I love to shop...but even as gutsy as I am, I stay the fuck home on Black Friday...and I gotta wonder why the niggers ain't up in arms over THIS term!

I just saw a new Energizer commercial...and the final line was "Do you have the Bunny inside?" I'll bet there are some real perverts out there seeing that commercial, and getting ideas. Isn't it bad enough they put hamsters and gerbils up their asses? Now Energizer is asking them if they have a rabbit up there. Who thinks this shit up?!

I don't know who the nigger in the Joe Boxer commercials is...but he will never, ever, land a serious role. In fact, unless gay dancing becomes really popular, these ads will likely be the last we ever see of him. I'm sure he's going to read this...and get pissed about being referred to as a nigger...but seriously, do you think I'd be afraid of him? "Hey Man! You don't know me! I ain't no nigger! I'll fuck you up!" Oh! Wow! What are you going to do? Dance in front of me and make me sick? How can anyone be intimidated by this lame ass?

Ever read "Archie" comics? Depends on your age I guess. But for those of you who have, consider this, Archie is the epitome of the "clean cut all-American kid", sugary sweet and wholesome. Makes you wanna gag right? Well, maybe he's not as wholesome as you may think. Consider this: He runs around with two girls(Veronica and Betty), Betty is the female Archie, the "girl next door" type, Veronica is the bitch. Always plotting shit. Probably a slut too. You also have Reggie, the bad-ass, or so he wanted to be. He was tougher than Archie though, probably could whip Archie's all-American ass if he really wanted to. Ok, so you have two pairs, Archie and Betty, Reggie and Veronica. Who else is in there? "Jughead", which we can only assume is a nickname, no parents would name their kid that. Jughead rhymes with Drughead, and for a good reason. The motherfucker eats constantly. I know

Teens can eat, but not like this. At least not eat like that and stay skinny as that. That means he's got to be a pot head, and probably does a little cocaine or crystal meth to keep his weight down. Now, consider this also, he is the only one without a "love interest". Or maybe not...he is always hanging around with his canine companion. Maybe he's into bestiality. Of course, sex also tends to work up an appetite, contributing to that problem, while burning off calories, helping to keep him thin.

I got really fed up with consumerism, and marketing a few years ago. I was so disgusted with the whole thing that I created a "Morbid Collectables" catalog. It was all fake shit that you can't really buy(although there were some good ideas in there), but I wrote it in such a way that people actually believed this shit was for sale. Which was the whole point. If you don't get it, tough. American's will buy ANYTHING! I've included the latest version of the catalog at the end of this book, which is sure to offend. That's a good thing, because the catalog not only shows the public's gullibility(in believing this shit is for real), but also that they are still uptight about shit. Trust me on this, if anything you've read so far has offended you, don't bother looking at the catalog. I showed an early copy of it to someone with a rather sick sense of humor, and she told me I was going to burn in hell for thinking that stuff up. I took that as a compliment. If I can offend a sick minded person, I'm doing really well.

Have you ever noticed that there aren't any midget cops? Or private detectives? Ever wonder why? I'd think they'd be great at those jobs. Imagine being caught shoplifting or something, and the cop that busted you was literally half your height? How could you live that one down in prison? "I hear officer Murphy busted you." "Uh, yeah." "Well, if a midget could take you into custody....you are MY bitch now!"

I know people are stupid, but even WE are still shaking our heads over this one; I've got this new supervisor at FedEx, we'll call her "M". And what an incompetent fukwit! Let me backtrack a minute, I changed positions at our terminal, I moved over to QA(Quality Assurance), basically dealing with any address issues, directions, bad barcodes, lost packages, ripped boxes, that kind of thing. So I'm actually dealing with customers again. Now, "M" just got "promoted" to be the QA supervisor. Her and I banged heads almost immediately. She has no idea how the whole place works(and if you are going to supervise an area of a company that deals directly with customers, you NEED to know how every department interacts with yours). Now, we have to fill out a shipping label called an "RTS" which is return to shipper. This is pretty much the last resort(or is supposed to be, I see it being used quite liberally), you have to put the terminal number, the reason for the RTS, date, and the obvious: return state and zip code. A manager("M") is supposed to initial it below our initials. Rose spotted a package with an RTS label on it, that had the state of "Detroit" written on it. She pointed this out to me, so I told her she should take it to "M"(since she HAD initialed it). She did, then recounted what happened to me. She walked into the office where "M" and several other people were, and said "Are you "M"?", "Yes.", "Which one of your brainiacs thinks Detroit is a state?" ("M" looked at it, and gave the name.) Then "M" said something that we are both still shaking our heads over, "Detroit, that's in Illinois(she pronounced it Illinoize) isn't it?" To which Rose replied, "No, it's in Michigan.", "M" said, "Well, I don't know, I'm not from the mid-west." At this point, Rose bit her tongue, but she was thinking, "I'm not even from this country and I know that!", someone else in the office said, "She is human, and people do make mistakes." To which the love of my life replied with, "Well, apparently there are way too many people around here making too many mistakes." And then walked back out of the office. Now, in case this went over your head, "M" is a manager in a multi-billion dollar shipping company, and doesn't know where Detroit is? I mean, it's not like CARS are made there or anything. It's not like Detroit is actually FAMOUS for anything, you NEVER hear about it on the news. Gimme a fucking break! How do these unqualified morons GET these jobs?

I saw one of those "pop-up" ads you just can't get away from if you patrol the net, it read, "Enter your e-mail address..." for some promotion or another, and I'm thinking to myself, I'd love to see some fucking truth in these pop-ups, just once....I'd like to see one that reads "Enter your e-mail address so we can spam the fuck out of you, cram your mailbox, and insure that you won't be getting any e-mail you may want to get."

Something I like to do, is try to open an account at a bank at the drive in window. When they tell me I have to come inside for that, I simply explain that I don't have that kind of time. I also make it a point to ask for fries when doing my drive up banking. I can be a real pain in the ass when I'm high and bored. That's when I really get off fucking with people, just to amuse myself.

Here we are America, still going to Hell, but now someone has stolen the fucking hand basket!

All right, a fucking blizzard hits Maryland, 26 inches of snow in two days, and the whole fucking state shuts down. Not only this, but our Governor, Robert Erlich, was up at Camp David with the Prez for the weekend. Now, just to let you know how bad shit is, Erlich spends 1 fucking day with Dubya, and comes out talking like him. He was talking about the storm(they couldn't call it a blizzard, because of the lack of 30+ MPH winds....over 2 feet of snow, the state shuts down, drifts of 3-4 feet just by the wind blowing, but it's not a fucking blizzard...) and he said something about "inappropriate vehicles" being on the road, "...but that got real better, real quick..." At this point, I knew he'd been hanging with the big D.

Speaking of the "Winter Storm" that couldn't be called a blizzard, Sunday morning, we woke up to see all the closings around the state....every mall in the state was closed. The shit wasn't even getting up to full speed yet! A storm this fucking huge, and NOBODY saw it coming?! They even banned private transportation for the day, no "unauthorized" vehicles could be on the road. And the funny part was, all the people who got stuck, most of them got stranded before this order came down. But you know the state is still going to slap them with the fine...anything for the almighty dollar.

Another thing that got me about this, was the fact that ALL local TV programming was pre-empted for two days over this..."It's snowing in Downtown Baltimore, let's go over to (so and so) in Westminster, what's it doing over there?" "It's snowing like hell here. Back to you in the studio." "Now let's check in with Catonsville." "Snowing like a motherfucker here, back to you!" "How about Owings Mills?" "Snowing here too..." You get the idea? 50 straight hours of this shit! If a fucking terrorist attack would have occurred sometime in there, even THAT would have been pre-empted. "Sorry, we are covering a major weather event here, no time for hundreds/thousands of deaths, we've got SNOW to report on!" All right, follow me a minute... everyone in the whole fucking state is snowed in...we are all prisoners to mother nature, and these fuckwits take off the shows we might want to see, just to show us why we can't fucking go anywhere?!

I just saw a good one on the news, some sparklers are being recalled, because they could "Catch fire and burn"...now, how bizarre is THAT? Sparklers that could burn...who'dathunkit?

Wanna clear out a black bar? Have a woman walk in with a child, and have the child yell, "Mommy, which one is my Daddy?"

"...For Dummies."....every fucking thing under the sun, "For Dummies"...Started out as a joke, when it was "Windows, For Dummies", it meant people new to it. It was lighthearted, it was a way of saying, "I'm new to computers, and I don't know anything about them." No big deal, it was a joke. Now, they've got a "For Dummies" book for everything. Maybe before I'm done with this book, I'll add "NOT for Dummies!" to the bottom of the title. The shit is ridiculous. I wonder if Bush has a book called "Politics, For Dummies".... he sure the fuck couldn't write one. He might be the subject of one, but he couldn't write one.

All right, it's a Sunday morning, and now we've seen it all. Talk about preying on the public's fears; now someone is selling a video on "How to protect yourself in case of a terrorist attack." Including wrapping a wet paper towel around your face after dipping it in baking soda, this will definitely protect you from a biological attack....and if you are dumb enough to believe this, you shouldn't be reading this book! Did I mention the part about wrapping your house in plastic? Why don't they start selling the bomb-shelters again? Remember those? Back during the "Cold War"? Fuckers sold like hot cakes, anything that can prey on your fears, and make a quick buck. One more thing, if this video is so vital to your survival, why are they SELLING it on TV, it's not available in stores though, but why are they selling it? Isn't this the kind of thing that the government should provide to you? Since they are SO concerned about our health and welfare?

And just when we THOUGHT we'd seen it all... flip the channel and get something else. Microwave cookware that changes colors so you know the food is done. If you are dumb enough to need the bowl to change colors so you know the food is done, you shouldn't be eating! And they are targeting ADULTS with this shit!!! And they even had the temerity(look it up fuckwad!) to say, "No more sticking your finger in the food in your microwave!" Tell me, how many times have you pulled something out of the microwave, and stuck your finger into it to see if it's hot enough to eat?

Not me, I usually stick my dick in there to see if it's hot enough.

Oh, the news was full of material this morning. Harvard University, or as I like to call it, Snob U, had an incident recently. A group of students(who have not been identified), created a nine foot tall snow penis(complete with testicles), then covered it with ice to prevent "shrinkage". A couple days later, a pair of female students(I'll get to them in a minute), in order to "prevent others from being offended" knocked the sculpture down. Just the fact that this story has taken place, is funny. I have a few comments about the story, which I hope are even funnier. First of all, I've seen a picture of it, and it seemed a little pointy at the top...not quite as symmetrical as say, mine. Anyway, a nine foot tall penis(which, going by my definition, makes it a cock) is, shall we say, typical of the male mentality...meaning that every male(with a few exceptions) is fairly not happy with their size. They all want it bigger...of course, they are dumb enough to not realize that anything larger would probably result in "You ain't putting that thing in ME!" This of course being said by either a male, or a female, depending on your persuasion. I don't know any fags that want a nine incher going into their assholes, let alone a nine FOOT one. Be that as it may, I have to wonder who actually made this sculpture, was this really male artistry? If so, and they used one their own for a model, that model needs surgery. But suppose for a moment, this was female artistry, how do those girls feel about destroying what had to be hours of work, done by some of their "sisters"? And speaking of the wreckers, there was a picture of them on the Harvard website, and several things struck me about them...the first thing being that they are a couple of fat, ugly, stuck-up looking cunts. Secondly, it's more than obvious that they have no sense of humour...if they had, they would have drawn smiley faces on the balls(this idea comes courtesy of Rose)... or maybe build a snow hand next to the penis. That would have been funny, as well as made a statement. Or maybe put a clear trash bag over it, and hung a sign about using rubbers on it(like "If the glove ain't there, you'll be fucking the air!") Show a little brains...no wait, these are college students, brains don't work for them, sorry.

Michael Jackson hired a voodoo "priest" to kill Steven Spielberg and David Geffen. A voodoo "priest" named Baba(now THERE'S a name I trust!)....he would have been better off to get Baba to resurrect John Gotti and paid him less to knock them off, then to hire a couple of voodoo nut jobs. The article I read about it says that Jackson has an "enemies list" that these two were(or are?) on, and that Geffen helped take down his career(couldn't have ANYTHING to do with the child molesting, oh no!), and that Spielberg refused to cast him in a new "Peter Pan" movie. I guess they didn't want to have to rename the movie to "Peter Plastic-Man". This in deference to Jackson being more plastic than biological at this point. Personally, I think he'd be better suited for an updated version of "Pinocchio"... only instead of a wooden puppet who wanted to be a boy, he could be a plastic man who wants to be with boys....oh wait, he is.

Getting back to the nine-foot snow penis, turns out it actually was done by males. Whoa! What a shocker there! Rose came up with another good "protest" idea for that, she told me they should have built a life sized one right next to it, and put up a sign pointing to both of them...the part pointing to the nine foot one would read "What men wish they had." And the one pointing to the life sized one, "What men DO have."

Oh BOY! The CIA, or whoever the fuck it was, has "arrested" the "brains behind the September 11th attack"...I'm thrilled. Hell, it only took a year and a half, and for some reason, I don't feel like it accomplished anything. Shit, this asshole has had that much time to train more fuckwits and get them in place. That's assuming he really is the brains behind the attacks. I wouldn't put it past the government to simply find a look-alike(well...that isn't all that difficult) and claim he is the one they were after. Of course, Bin Laden is still running loose. Speaking of Bin Laden...did anyone notice back during the attacks(and even since) that there were TWO spellings of his first name? CNN and most of the other networks were spelling it "Osama", while MSNBC and that bunch were spelling it "Usama"...kinda like the shit with Elvis...was his middle name "Aron" or "Arron"? MAKE UP YOUR FUCKING MINDS!

Speaking of Elvis...a few years ago, I had at least 300 people believing that Elvis was alive up until the 25th anniversary of his death(or, for you fuckwads who believe he IS still alive, disappearance)...All the radio stations were playing Elvis...you couldn't get away from the shit. First of all, Elvis DID revolutionize music in his time...no argument there...but he wasn't THAT good! Anyway, since I love to fuck with people, I decided to have some fun that day. I was still working at the liquor store, and got to talk to hundreds of people. I told them all, and very convincingly I might add, that Elvis was on his way back to the US from his hiding spot in Canada, and that his plane crashed, and that all aboard were killed. I presented it with a fair bit of acting, and everyone I told this to believed me! I'm not joking! Of course I noted the irony of the story that after faking his death, and going into hiding for 25 years, that on the day he had set up to return, he was killed. If nothing else, it's more proof of the typical American gullibility!

One night while working at FedEx, I was unloading a van, and ran across a spliced box. It was actually two boxes taped together so the contents would fit, but the thing that struck me as funny, is that both boxes had "This end up!" written on them, with arrows for the stupid, but they both pointed in opposite directions! How fucking bright was this idiot?

I recently saw in the paper, that someone was charged with "...carrying a deadly weapon with intent to injure." My question is, what constitutes "intent to injure"? And exactly how does one classify a "deadly weapon"? To me, deadly weapons include nuclear missiles, machine guns, chemical weapons, biological weapons, knives, razors, handguns, rifles, shotguns, catapults, forks, spoons, pens, pencils, cars/trucks/etc, household chemicals, bombs, firecrackers, sparklers, sticks, boards, nails, screws, any tool you can name, books, planes, lighters, oil, gasoline, matches, paint, glass, even paper! Hell, I can't even list all the shit that could be a weapon! That would be a book in and of itself! The point is, bare hands can be deadly, and anything in the right hands could be a deadly weapon. Fuck, who needs a gun store? You can pick up all you need down at the dollar store!

Dollar stores, I remember when we had the old "Five and Dime" stores...you could walk out of that place with an armload of shit for a buck!

We've got this black guy over at work, his name is Jason, and he's really cool! I'm sure he'll be happy with me mentioning his name in here, but who cares. Anyway, he was walking past where I was working, so I called him over and asked him, "Hey Jason, does your mother know you are dressing like a Honkey?" Before he could say anything, I pressed the issue a little, "Tell me, do you dress like a Honkey because your friends dress like Honkey's? Or is it because you actually LIKE it?" He started laughing, shook his head, and walked away. Speaking of work, I did something I'd been threatening to do for a while. I mentioned that we have to go through a little guard shack(like these people scare me!) And we get the pat-down, and the metal detector routine. Well, I threatened to do something really ignorant one night...and they finally pushed me far enough. I was rather pissed anyway, the heating in the main part of the building had gone out, and we almost left within an hour after getting there. But anyway, there is a camera up in one corner of the shack, so I jumped up on the counter there, pointed my ass at the camera, and dropped my pants. Then wiggled my ass for the camera, and both of the security guards almost died! They freaked out big time. It was funny as shit. Rose kept telling them, "You asked for it!"

Speaking of the guards, during the day, there is only one guy there, and we were just coming in on Valentine's day. He was standing outside smoking a cigarette, and made a comment about how I should have brought him something for Valentine's Day, like a kiss. I reached for the back of his neck to pull him in for a big smooch on the nose, and he hauled ass! As I started to reach behind him, he ducked, turned and bolted like someone had just zapped him with 60,000 volts. Rose almost pissed herself laughing. The dude was really freaked out. He didn't even search us that day.

I mentioned the Osborne's TV show earlier, and now the entire first season is out on DVD, so I bought it. I love that show, and talk about a deal, close to eight hours of footage, and without the beeps. Although, one thing that I find rather annoying about it, is while they let the language fly(which I fully fucking support!), but they blur out anytime Ozzy gives the finger...what the fuck?! Stone Cold gives the double finger on the WWF broadcasts, and they don't blur HIM out! And yes, I know it's now the WWE, but FUCK THEM!

The news was ripe today, CBS is going to do a "Beverly Hillbilly's" style reality show. Assuming he's not behind it, I'd bet Jeff Foxworthy is either freaking out, or calling a lawyer, maybe both.

"It shows just how shallow of a country we are living in when there is more focus on what the nominees are wearing to the Oscars than how qualified the nominees are to win an award." -Rose

I think I'm going to be calling one of the local talk radio stations in the next day or so, I'm going to air this here, but people need to be made aware of this one, and sooner than this book will be published. But some fuckwit in Israel is selling "Terror Tours" of the West Bank and Gaza Strip. I swear this is true! I happened to find out about it on the BBC website, which I'm going to be checking a lot more! The tour offers, among other things, "Aerial tours of 'terrorist' enclaves, and a chance to sit in the cockpit of a fighter plane capable of delivering nuclear bombs." This is a four day excursion, that refers to the "highlight" of the trip to be: "A paintball fight in a simulated Arab village, where participants will be able to go from room-to-room 'cleaning out Arab terrorists'." This at a cost of $5,500 each. Now, correct me if I'm wrong here, but suppose, just suppose, a German had done this same thing, offering the same exact attractions, but instead of Arab Terrorists, it was labeled as "Jewish Citizens", or maybe a Palestinian had conceived the idea, and used an "Israeli Village" instead...Israel would be bombing the fuck out of someone! Hell, let's try that one here in the states, and have the tour given by the KKK, seeking out "uppity negro's"! I bet THAT would go over good!!! Or maybe just offer Whites the chance to hunt down and "kill"(via simulation of course) some of the formerly numerous Native American Tribes...same fucking thing! And I bet I'll be labeled an anti-semite for this suggestion! Fuck you.

I heard a frightening new term this morning, and I can see where this one will go, this will turn into another fucking reality show. Parents are going to go fucking nuts over this one, claiming their child is one. God help us, here come the "Baby Diva's"!

"Old Faithful" was designed and built by space aliens to be a natural clock, hence it's regularity, trust me, it's not because they dump Metamucil into it.

I love this, every time you turn around, they've got some simple minded "cure" for some stupid shit, now they are talking about taking aspirin to help prevent colon cancer, of course, you may have to tolerate internal bleeding and diarrhea. I think I'll take the cancer, call me weird, but I prefer to leave any bleeding to the external portions of my anatomy, where I know about it.

Speaking of side affects, that "Gotta Go" commercial, for incontinence, you take such and such, and "I don't have to go right now"...of course, there are the potential side affects, which include; dry mouth, abdominal pain, constipation, and headaches. Personally, I'd rather buy a box of diapers, that way, the only thing I have to worry about is the potential embarrassment of asking someone to change me. I think they need a commercial about Diarrhea, using the same tune, "Gotta shit, gotta shit, gotta shit right now..." You don't need a drug to be the focal point, this could be an ad for Depends.

Tony Blair, the British prime minister, has stated "Saddam could either use weapons of mass destruction directly, or provide them to terrorist organizations for future use..." Makes him sound dangerous, doesn't it? That's what they want, to make Saddam sound dangerous. He's less of a threat to the US than 300 fags who took beauty lessons and have attitude problems.

Here's something else to think about, I didn't see anyone in Europe decrying when the US was "providing arms to insurgents" in Central America. Isn't that what happened? The US provided arms to a group of people intent on overthrowing the legitimate governments of several countries, including supporting the Taliban in Afghanistan(this during their fight against the Russians). Sounds like the kind of shit they are saying Saddam COULD do, not HAS done, but has the potential to do. And for those of you who STILL think the US is always in the right, consider that our military STILL has stockpiles of nerve gas hidden somewhere.

From the "People who take themselves WAY too seriously" file: A French Chef(allegedly one of France's best), named Bernard Loiseau committed suicide because his restaurant might drop down a place or two in the "Gault-Millau Guide". I wonder what he would have done had he found out it would have fallen OFF the list?

And to prove that Religion STILL doesn't have a sense of humour, the Kentucky Mountain Bible College was granted a new phone number, because their old one started with the prefix "666".

Also in the news, during his interview with Dan Rather, Saddam Hussein challenged Dubya to a debate. Of course, Dubya declined...since Saddam has a better command of the English language than he does. IMHO, Saddam should have been worried that Dubya MAY accept, just so the FBI can kill him.

From the "Only in America" file: There is a proposal in Maryland to allow "Undocumented Immigrants"(Read: Illegal Aliens!) to legally obtain a drivers license...while retaining their illegal immigrant status! What the fuck!? And they have support of people in the State Legislature! You aren't going to believe this, but a member of the American Immigration Lawyers Association told the committee looking at this proposal, "...This bill is not ideal, but they watch our kids. They clean our houses. ...If there were a mass deportation, our economy would collapse." Correct me if I'm wrong here, but if they are working illegally, they aren't paying taxes, which means they are getting away with something even the BEST of us can't get away with. Don't misunderstand me here, this bill does have opposition, and I support that! The part that gets me though, is where the fuck was the INS when this meeting was held, and why didn't they nab the dozens of them who were at this hearing? Talk about an opportunity to round up part of the border patrol's fuck ups!

"An American Airlines pilot was arrested and accused of threatening security personnel at an airport checkpoint. He allegedly told them that he had an ax in the cockpit, and would chop off their heads. He did not return calls seeking additional comment." What kind of comments were they looking for? That he was going to sexually abuse the bodies afterward? That he had found a really good recipe on the internet and wanted a substitute for chicken? What the fuck?!?!

A friend of mine recently said to me, "An idle mind is John's workshop." I couldn't agree more! Thanks Jewel.

Something else to ask, why do Mothers get all the fucking attention? Anytime you see some idiot on TV, it's always "HI MOM!!", they never mention Dad. Always Moms. "Your Momma", "Motherfucker", always about the mothers. Just once, I'd like to see someone on TV stand up and yell, "HI DAD! You wife beating bastard! You alcoholic asshole!" Just give your pop some recognition! Course, we know why the niggers never do that, but honkeys have no excuse.

I once freaked out a coworker, he was dating the store owner's daughter, and I pointed out to him, "Everytime you kiss her, you are kissing her daddy's cum." He hasn't been the same since.

For those of you wondering, we worship the great God "Ganja", and I grant you, we don't have a trinity, but we do have a duality. Along with the God "Ganja", we have the "Virgin Mary Juana."

Burt Aaronson, a Florida politician, is leading a campaign to change the name of "French Fries"(which aren't French at all, but what can you expect from one of Bush's cronies?), to "Freedom Fries", because he's pissed off at France. I'm actually surprised that no one came up with this sales ploy after 9-11. I can see it now, they come in a handy "Bomber Pack", similar to a kids meal, but shaped like several of the air force's most notable planes. And, as a side note, for those of you stupid enough to think that French fries really originated in France, look to Belgium for the truth. He's also pissed at the Germans for their supporting the French in their probable veto of the UN resolution. I guess that means Hamburgers(Hamburg, Germany) will have to change their name too, and Frankfurters(Frankfurt, Germany)as well. Of course, the Burgers could be named "Mystery-Meat-Patties"(now there would be some truth in advertising!), and the Franks could simply be referred to as "Wienies"...Oh wait, that's the title of this dipshit and his cronies.

During the first ever "Cat Pride March" in Rome, Italy, a photo was taken of a man dressed as a Roman Gladiator(also known as a Trojan) holding up a cat. My first thought to seeing this picture was, "That Trojan is way too big for that pussy!"

Dubya must be a big Dr. Seuss fan, one unit of the marines over near Iraq has the name, "Big Fish, Little Fish". I'm wondering though, do they dig fish ponds instead of foxholes?

I tell you what, I'd hate to be in that outfit, could you imagine writing home to your parents? They are liable to have to recalled and sent to either rehab, or a psycho ward.

From the "You can't please ANYONE!" file: Several convicted murderers were given life(or multiple life) sentences. Of course, the group using racial disparity in sentencing are up in arms over these decisions. Meanwhile, no one is pointing out to them that the "Anti-Death Penalty" crowd(made up by mostly the same people) are pushing a "moratorium" on the death penalty.

What the fuck is going on here? Nearly a dozen people were arrested and charged with disorderly conduct, as well as assaulting a police officer, during a high school fashion show. What the hell happened? Did two women show up wearing the same outfit? Did someone make a snide comment about someone else's shoes? What the fuck?!?!

In North Dakota, the new Emergency Hotline that was installed in the Governor's office rang three times in it's first week of operation. Of course, they were not emergency calls, one was a wrong number, the other two were telemarketers. I'm just wondering if one of those telemarketers was calling from one of those security companies.

A police officer pulled over a car with stolen tags. After doing a search of the vehicle, arrested the driver and charged him with larceny of tags, and possession of cocaine. Then they released him on his own recognizance.

Here's one from the newsroom: The local news cut into a news broadcast about the Shuttle disaster to report on, the Shuttle disaster!

Someone actually stole a radiator from an "earth moving machine" parked at an equipment rental place. Tell me, what the fuck are they going to do with it? Somehow, I doubt it's going to turn up in a local pawn shop. Although, I suppose with enough cleaning, it could make a huge water bong. I just don't see this as the kind of thing a Stoner would do. A Crack head, maybe, but not a Stoner.

We got a Ferret last year, they are really cool pets, too. The dog is afraid of her though, which is really funny when you realize that the dog is a Yellow-Lab/Sheppard mix. I've walked past the ferret's cage on several occasions, and seen her sleeping in her hammock. She's obviously dreaming about something, and I often stand there and wonder what it might be.

Do people who have sex with blow-up dolls do foreplay? Do they give the doll oral sex? And if so, WHY?!

I heard something recently that I find more than mildly ironic: Public schools are being fined $100.00 per day that their water fountains are usable. Apparently the lead level of the water in these fountains is "unacceptable". Of course, the schools already can't afford to have enough books for the kids, nor can they afford to pay for decent teachers. But they are not going to have a problem coming up with that kinda money for these fines, because it doesn't matter if the kids don't have enough books, most of them can't read anyway.

I just heard about a Marine who was forced to choose between his duty to his family, and his duty to "his country". His son was in the hospital, getting a heart transplant when he got called up. He chose to go to Iraq. Wrong choice, asshole. Family comes first, always. If that was my son, I'd have been at that hospital the whole time. No one or nothing would have torn me away. Think about this too, suppose he gets killed over there(where he doesn't belong to begin with, but that's my opinion, not Dubya's). Can you hear his kid as a teenager? "Mom, tell me again how Dad chose to kill people who were no threat to us, instead of being at my side when I needed him as a baby."

I wanna see that goof from the Joe Boxer commercials and Vin Diesel make a gay porn movie.

I walked into my bank one day, sat the withdrawal slip on the counter, and said, "This ain't a stick up, gimme all my money." The teller was not amused.

If, by now, I have not managed to offend you in some way, I apologize.

At one time, Christianity was considered a cult.

From the "They musta been rasslin fans" department: Two thieves, one armed with a handgun, attempted to rob a Chinese restaurant. They both fled when an employee threatened them with a chair.

If James Moran Jr. ran for President, I'd vote for him. But only if he takes back the apology.

The General in charge of the Iraqi invasion, is named Tommy Franks. Why is it that a General named "Tommy" doesn't scare me? Although, I can easily see Dubya asking to talk to "Tommy" about "Big Fish, Little Fish."

Note to the BBC: You've been listening to Bush talk too much. I recently saw on your website the following: "The professional military view here is that once any war begins it will be fought to its inevitable conclusion whatever happens."

Rose and I finally left FedEx, we'd finally had enough. Now we are working at a Greenhouse/Nursery. Talk about the coolest job in the world! Granted, as of this writing, we've only been there a couple of weeks, but for the most part, all the people there are pretty cool, and the job is perfect for us. Look for more info on this, and later stuff in my next work, which I'll be starting before this one is published. Yes, you may cringe in fright now.

This may come as a shock to you, but I am completely against the "War in Iraq". But something I really feel I need to say on this, is that you "SuperPatriots" are really getting to be a pain in the ass. You all bitch about the protesters, and call them "UnAmerican", "Saddam Lovers", all kinds of shit. Fuck you. I can't speak for ALL of these people, but from the ones I've talked to, we are all in the same boat. We don't hate the troops fighting this "war", far from it. We want to see them come home safe, we just don't believe they should be there in harms way in the first place. We blame the Bush administration for putting them there, where they can get killed. The soldiers are doing what they were programmed to do, and what they are TOLD to do. Nothing more. They aren't responsible for being there. It's the fuckwits in charge that I have a problem with. So, for those of you who feel the need to call us all sorts of names, simply for voicing our opinion, YOU are the traitors. YOU are the ones who are the anti-Americans. YOU support censorship, and denial of freedoms. So to you, I say, GET THE FUCK OUT.

Someone recently commented to me about being a pessimist. I told her that "I'm not a pessimist, I'm a cynic. Pessimism requires caring."

A thought just came to me, we already have Chief Moose...I think we need a Deputy Squirrel. Can you hear the criminals now? "We must avoid Moose and Squirrel!"

According to the American and British military, the "War in Iraq" is "Going as planned." Does this include all the deaths and woundings due to "friendly fire"? And if this was part of the plan, WHY?!

Wouldn't it be funny if all those organ donors found out that they couldn't get into heaven while some of their body parts are still alive?

"Actualulety" is another word that tells you that your brain has stopped functioning, but your mouth has not.

I wonder when "bathrooms" or "restrooms" are going to be replaced with "Human Waste Disposal Centers".

I heard a REAL good one on the news, and this one tells me just what kinds of morons are running this "war"... "The battle is over, but the fighting is still going on." Can someone explain this one to me?

The FBI runs a national database of criminals/terrorists/fugitives/etc...BUT they aren't required to ensure the accuracy of said database...WHAT THE FUCK?!

Let's see, once we are through with Iraq, who's next on the list? The Syrians? Russians? Israel? Pakistan? North Korea? The first two are already on our shit list, for allegedly supplying arms to the Iraqis(not that the US ever did such a thing, Saddam only has a "key" to ONE U.S. city...Detroit). Israel, well, don't they have "weapons of mass destruction", including nukes? And they are in violation of a couple of U.N. resolutions also!

There are still "terrorists" in Pakistan, why not invade them? North Korea is developing nukes, guess they are on the list of potential targets as well. And how about Iran? They have oil...let's take that too! And since we are on this whole "Conquer the Evils of the World" kick, let's go ahead an invade Canada, just because they have part of Niagara Falls in their territory, and a better health care system. They are embarrassing us. Let's attack! Hell, let's even go after the guy who laid claim to the territory on the Moon! He owns it, and since we don't know what all natural resources are on the moon, let's kill him and take that too! At least it will keep it out of the hands of the terrorists!

Here's a quote of something disturbing I read, "...we will not allow our war plan to be stymied by concern for our prisoners of war." If this doesn't make you wanna protest in Washington against the war, you are a bigger idiot than I thought.

From the "He learned from Americans very well" department, a Russian Tycoon is being charged with defrauding a regional government. Naturally, he claims to have done nothing illegal.

A US Army Sergeant may go to trial for tossing a couple of grenades into an American command tent. His name, oddly enough, is Asan Akbar. Gee, does that name sound slightly ARABIC? I'm just waiting to see if the families of the (as I write this) two soldiers who died in that attack, if they will be doing the usual talk-show circuit. And if they do, will the parents of Akbar be doing them as well? I doubt it, seeing as how the CIA or someone probably has them off somewhere being interrogated as potential terrorists.

From Rome, Italy: a costumed troupe of Gladiators is being forcibly removed from the Coliseum. Apparently, these people dress up like the old Romans and pose for pictures with tourists. According to the article I saw(Reuters web site), the Rome Council once threatened to impose regulations on these people, who wear(according to the Council) "cheap costumes and carry plastic swords"...a regulation to make their costumes more authentic. Are they actually proposing having these people carry REAL swords? Then they will probably claim they are "armed and dangerous" and have them locked up.

I wonder if protesting Israel's actions in regard to refugee camps counts as "Anti-Semetic"?

So much for that whole "Protect the Children" bullshit...the Republicans shot down a legislation known as the "Amber Alert" system. I'm sure you know what the Amber Alert thing is all about...it's a good thing. It will tell people about a child kidnapping that can be stopped before the perpetrator can kill the child. Of course, the Republican's probably couldn't make any money off of it, so of course, it goes down.

Heh, check this out...the very lawmakers who have outlawed prayer in schools, are now pushing for a "national day of prayer/fasting". So much for the separation of church and state.

Rose and I were talking one night about our "after life" plans. I told her that I'd like to be planted someplace nice. She told me that she wanted to be cremated. I looked her right in the eyes and asked, "What is it with you Germans and putting people in ovens?" She replied, "I just want to follow in my Fuehrer's footsteps."

Rose was diagnosed with Ovarian cancer. I won't get into the details, but she ended up going through surgery for it. If you've ever been through surgery, you know that right before they wheel you into the O.R., you get a parade of people who are going to be working on you. This is not always reassuring. In fact, this can be very disturbing. For example, the anesthesiologist was Jewish….he walked over wearing his yarmulke…. which did not go very well with the green scrubs he was wearing….which at least told me he wasn't gay. Anyway, he's Jewish….Rose is German. I'm sitting there, and the first thought that went through my head was, "Shit, I hope this guy isn't holding a grudge over that little 'Holocaust' thing!" Of course, he wasn't. Then you get to meet the nurses, interns, and finally, the surgeon. Now, I don't normally succumb to shock, or surprise easily….but I did when I saw the surgeon. If you've ever seen the show "OZ", the prison show on HBO, the surgeon looks just like the character; McMannis, the administrator of "Emerald City" on the show. I'm sitting there thinking, "Well fuck, it could be worse… he could look like one of the INMATES!" Anyway, the surgery went well, but she had an incision about 2 feet long on her stomach, and they don't stitch you up anymore…they staple you up. Looked like she had a giant zipper on her torso. As a result of this, she could not laugh for two weeks, because it hurt so bad. Now, you really have to feel sorry for her. Imagine, looking at me naked, first thing in the morning, and NOT being able to laugh. I bet none of YOU could do it! This was a week or so before Christmas, and a few days after

Christmas, one of our friends came over, and this will tell you why Rose and I are such a perfect match, he asked what she got for Christmas, to which she replied, "Carved up like a Christmas Ham." and pulled up her shirt a little to show the scar with the staples holding it together. A few weeks later, she had to go in again, for this thing called a "Port-A-Catheter." They use this little thing so they don't have to keep re-sticking the same vein for the Chemo. We were waiting in the pre-op, right before the usual parade starts up again, and overheard someone being told "You won't have much make-up left after the surgery." I got to thinking, "Who the fuck is so vain that they feel the need to put on make-up for surgery?!" Get a fucking grip, people!! These doctors don't give a shit what you look like on the outside, it's the INSIDE they are concerned with!!!

The biggest thing I want everyone to realize, is that I hate people in general, because they are selfish, narrow-minded, and greedy. They generalize, label, and take advantage of others because they have some minor difference in appearance, lifestyle, or belief. Those of you who do not fall into the category of the "typical human being", by treating people as individuals, and not lumping them into a predetermined category defined by someone else, you are the people I have no problems with and it is for you that this book was intended. You know who you are.

And now, as promised, The Morbid Collectables Catalog.

Morbid Collectibles
Updated 03/11/2K2

Oklahoma City Bombing Merchandise

Item #100357 *Building Brick Fragments*- Now you can own a piece of history. These authentic bricks come to us from the Oklahoma City Demolition Company, and were once a part of the Edward R. Murrow building which was destroyed by a bomb blast in 1996. The bombing leveled 25% of the building, killed hundreds of people, and shocked the nation. Be the first on your street to own one of these rare bricks. Each brick comes with a certificate of authenticity. We have four styles to choose from, but hurry, these items are in limited quantities.

#100357-A : Standard Brick	$19.95
#100357-B : Brick with Blood Stains	$39.95
#100357-C : Brick with Bombing Residue	$39.95
#100357-D : Brick with both Blood Stains and Bombing Residue	$69.95

Item #100368 *Oklahoma: The Bombing*- This 3 hour documentary features 90 minutes of pure mayhem of the blast as well as rescue efforts, along with footage not seen on ANY newscast. You will witness first hand, the blast as seen through the eyes of Joe Watson, amateur reporter with a handy camcorder. You will also see heroics of normal people called into hazardous rescue duties, without even getting paid for it! Plus, order with your credit card, and get a FREE video tape! The Making of the Bomb! This exclusive video gives a detailed account of how Timothy McVie and Terry Nichols acquired the materials, the formula, and how they put it all together. The first 500 people ordering will receive a signed and numbered copy, complete with certificate of authenticity.

#100368-A : Oklahoma:The Bombing VHS $29.95

#100368-B : Oklahoma:The Bombing DVD $44.95

World War II Collectibles

Item#026755 *MoNAZIly-* Play Monopoly as you never have before. Instead of standard, boring streets, this game gives you concentration camps! For utilities, we offer a Genetic-Engineering Lab & a Tiger Tank Factory. The railroads are still there, because they were used to transport Jews from their homes to the camps. Community Chest is gone, but replaced with "Jew Did It." Chance has been slightly altered to "No Chance." "Read Mein Kampf" has replaced Free Parking, and "The Cooler" has replaced In Jail. The game starts out using German Marks for currency, however, only Jews can be used to pay rent, taxes, etc...so be prepared to trade in those Marks for Jews! Houses and Hotels are gone, replaced with "Ovens" and "Gas Chambers."

#026755 MoNAZIly Board Game $26.95

Item #026790 *"Run For Your Kike" Video Game-* This strategy based game puts you in charge of a Nazi concentration camp. It's up to you to build the camp, it's defenses, capacity, post guards, etc...but you know, not everything can go as planned. As with the camps in real life, Jews are always looking to escape, and allied forces are looking to help them. You have to keep the prisoners where they belong. But remember, while new ones are coming in, you have to make room for them. And spies can be among any load of prisoners you get, so be sure to 'cleanse' the camp often.

#026790 Run For Your Kike- The Video Game. Mac/Windows CD $29.95

Item #026799 *Human Skin Lampshades*- These authentic, hand made lampshades were originally crafted in Germany in 1942-1944. German prison camps produced these high quality lampshades during WWII! A perfect Hanukkah gift! Own a piece of history(or your family tree!) with this item!

#026799 Human Skin Lampshades $19.95

Item #026821 *"Another Look at Adolf Hitler" Video*- Power monger, or misunderstood practical joker? You be the judge! This 90 minute biography will take you from his humble beginnings as a half-Jew outcast, through his teen years of struggling to find a source of pork chops, and pouring kosher wine down the toilet, into his adult years giving the German people a leader they should be proud of.

#026821 "Another Look at Adolf Hitler" Video. (VHS Only) $14.95

Item #026837 *"Mein Kampf"- Limited Edition*- This is a FIND!! Once Germany was reunited, these rare books resurfaced. Once thought destroyed by the Russian Army, these highly collectable books were actually hidden deep within a German bunker. 500 copies of Mein Kampf, signed and numbered by the author, Adolf Hitler himself, made their way to a Swiss Auction, and we grabbed them all. Why? To make them available to YOU! The handwriting has been verified to be authentic, and we are offering a certificate of authenticity with each copy. Mein Kampf was printed in 1940, and is in it's original German format. Also, just to sweeten an already sweet deal, we are offering the English version! ABSOLUTELY FREE!!!(With purchase of the limited edition). You will find these books nowhere else!

#026837-A Mein Kampf- Limited Edition w/English version. $579.95

#026837-B Mein Kampf- English Edition $19.95

Item #026925 *Hitler's Mustache!* That's right! We have it! The most famous lip-hair ever! According to the Russian Government, before burning Hitler's body, a Russian General shaved off THE most recognizable mustache in history! When we found out this item was going up for bid, we spared NO expense to get it! This one of a kind item is forever sealed in a Plexiglas case. Each hair perfectly arranged in their original order.

#026925 Hitler's Mustache $125,000.00

Death Row Collectibles

Item #107480 *Death Row Signature Series Trading Cards-* We contracted the most well known death row inmates to create these high quality cards, THEN had them sign and number them! Each card comes in a hard plastic case, with certificate of authenticity! All cards have been hand signed by the killer they display! A MUST for any collector! Available individually only.

#107480-A Charles Manson(#1-500) $19.95

#107480-B Jeffrey Dahmer(#1-307) (He was killed before finishing 500) $24.95

#107480-C David Berkawitz(#1-500) (Son of Sam) $19.95

#107480-D Sam Shepard(#1-500) (Hillside Strangler) $19.95

Item #107503 *Jeffrey Dahmer Paring Knife-* This hand crafted knife is perfect for the serial killer who cares! This knife will take skin off of bone so fast your hands won't get bloody! It even goes through tough muscle like lightning! At this price, it's a bargain!

#107503 Jeffrey Dahmer Paring Knife $14.95

How-To Books and Videos

Item #370261 *Hypnotism Made Easy-* What do Charles Manson, Jim Jones, and David Koresh have in common? They bought this easy to follow, step-by-step system! This complete book and video course will teach you how to find, recruit, train and keep followers! Be your own boss! Hell, be your own Savior! Be the man everyone you know comes to for advice, money, and weapons! Teach your followers basic survival skills, how to spot prime targets for recruitment, and how to pull them away from nosey and controlling family members! You can be the envy of religious leaders throughout the world! Learn what concepts work, and which do not! You will be familiarized with how to acquire and store weapons, as well as how to set up a tax-free retreat, the best modes of travel to safely bring your followers in, and believe it or not, tactics that can keep the ATF at bay for months on end! You will not believe the bargain you are getting with this one!

#370261 Hypnotism Made Easy book and video $99.95

Item #370385 *Militia's Made Easy-* Similar to Hypnotism Made Easy, except with this course, you learn how to create a Militia Group! Learn basic weapon safety, advanced assault tactics, weapons storage and smuggling, as well as tax shelters to make the government pay for it all!

#370385 Militia's Made Easy book and video $99.95

NEW!!!!

Item #578036 *Trench Coat Mafia- The Video!* Follow the rampage in this never before seen footage! This tape was recovered from the house of a member of the Trench Coat Mafia! Guaranteed Authentic! This camera wielding maniac followed the teens through the massacre, catching every shot, bomb blast, and terrified student in crisp detail. Watch as cocky jocks are brought to their knees begging for mercy! See petrified Wiggers pleading for their lives! And, don't forget, the fateful blast that had one parent screaming racism! You will witness the shooting spree from the eyes of those who did the deed! And, if you act fast, you will also receive a limited copy of TCM- The Making of the Massacre! Included in this special video is the original play depicting the slaughter of classmates! Along with never before seen clips of the security camera's view of the cafeteria, and the library. PLUS, every tape from every 911 call to go out concerning this incident, with subtitles!

#578036 Trench Coat Mafia- The Video! **ONLY** $24.95

Item # 578042 *The TCM Starter Kit-* This exclusive item for the Pre-Teen Outcast includes a plastic trench coat, semi automatic BB gun, targets that look like schoolmates, and cap-loaded pipe bombs(50 caps included!) The plastic trench coat features the TCM logo on the back, and the pipe bombs use any standard cap-gun cap!

#578042 TCM Starter Kit $19.95

Item #578053 *The TCM Teen/Adult Kit-* Tired of always being singled out? Tired of the abuse? Tired of the beatings? Well, get even with your tormentors! This Teen/Adult Kit features a full length black Duster(With the TCM logo embroidered on the back!), 1 Semi-Automatic rifle, 200 rounds of ammunition, and 2 pipe bombs! All included for one LOW price!

#578053 TCM Teen/Adult Kit $239.95

Item #578061 *TCM T-Shirts!* These licensed T-Shirts are 50/50 cotton blend. Very high quality, and carry a 1-year warrantee! We have 6 different shirts available. Each shirt is available in black only.

#578061-A "I Survived the TCM Massacre!" Without bullet holes! $14.95

#578061-B "I Survived the TCM Massacre!" With Bullet holes! $19.95

#578061-C "My Psycho Kid Blew Away Your Honor Student!"
w/Bumper Sticker $14.95

#578061-D "Trench Coat Mafia" w/TCM Logo! $14.95

#578061-E "Property of the Trench Coat Mafia Training Facility" $14.95

#578061-F "Somebody went to Columbine High School and all I got
was this Shirt" $14.95

Item #578069 *Trench Coat Mafia Massacre: The Video Game!* Now in the works, and available on 07/04/99! Advance orders only! This game will be a first person shoot'em up for one or two players. It also features hidden levels, multiple school settings, and 5 levels of difficulty. You will be scored on kills, woundings, accuracy, and difficulty. More information on the game will be available as the release date approaches!

#578069-A Trench Coat Mafia Massacre: The Video Game N64 $65.95

#578069-B Trench Coat Mafia Massacre: The Video Game Sony $59.95

#578069-C Trench Coat Mafia Massacre: The Video Game DrmCst $59.95

#578069-D Trench Coat Mafia Massacre: The Video Game PC-CD $49.95

Item #595008 *Jolly Time Home Suicide Kit-* Are you sick and tired of being teased at school? Are you at your wits end dealing with insanely restrictive parents? Show them!

Kill yourself! And this easy to use kit will show you how! Included are 3 suicide pills, plus a guide to show you how to commit suicide 50 different ways! You choose your way out! Want to make a mess for them to clean up? Want to take a few of them with you? Want to make your most hated rival suspect #1? We'll show you how!

#595008 Jolly Time Home Suicide Kit! $69.95

Item #595105 *Disney Assault- The Video Game!* This game crosses two opposite worlds, as you get to suit up, and play as a member of the Trench Coat Mafia and attack Disney World, and Disney Land! Over 50 weapons, 35 levels, and hidden stages! Beat the game, and you can play as Eric Harris and Dillon Klebold in the awesome Multi-Player Mode!!

#595105-A Disney Assault- The Video Game N64	$59.95
#595105-B Disney Assault- The Video Game Sony	$49.95
#595105-C Disney Assault- The Video Game DrmCst	$59.95
#595105-D Disney Assault- The Video Game PC/CD	$39.95

THIS STUFF JUST IN!!

World Trade Center Merchandise

Item #672081 *Firehouse 17 Commemorative Poster!* This framed poster commemorates the failed rescue efforts of the crew of Firehouse 17. Without whose help, the death toll might have been lower. This MC Exclusive comes SIGNED and sealed in a protective, yet highly attractive oakwood frame. Signed by who? None other than the survivors of Firehouse 17, all three of them.

#672081 Firehouse 17 Commemorative Poster $79.95

Item #672136 *Pin the Beard on the Terrorist Game!* The perfect kids party game! Line up the 18 terrorist faces, blindfold the kids, and let them loose with the beards. Very similar to the classic 'pin the tail on the donkey' game, but styled for the new millennium!

#672136 - Pin the Beard on the Terrorist Game $19.95

Item #672155 *Turban Targets!* Tired of shooting skeet with ordinary clay-pigeons? Well surprise your buddies at the range with a set of these babies! These clay turbans meet or exceed all NRA Skeet Target requirements! A must have!

#672155A - Turban Targets (Box of 25) $29.95
#672155B - Turban Targets (Box of 50) $54.95
#672155C - Turban Targets (Gross of 144) *BEST VALUE* $99.95

Item #672316 *WTC Twin Towers Puzz3-D M.E.!* This 3 dimensional puzzle kit comes complete with floor plans, diagrams, and stands over 5 feet high! All 110 floors of each tower have been carefully crafted, and include miniature people, office furniture, the works! Also, in this special Millennium Edition, you also get 2 scale model 757 airliners, and a box of smoke bombs so that you may recreate the events of Sept. 11, 2001 anytime you want!

#672316 - WTC Twin Towers Puzz3-D M.E. $69.95

Item #672438 *Commemorative Plane Tickets!* These are actual unsold tickets for American Airlines Flights # 11 and # 77 , as well as United Airlines Flights # 93 and # 175. Each set comes framed with a certificate of authenticity, and the caption "Ride into Destiny! 09-11-01"

#672438 Commemorative Plane Tickets $139.95

Item #672509 *Do-It-Yourself Hijacking Kit!* Just added to our line of Do-It-Yourself aids, this hijacking kit comes ready to use! This kit comes with glue-on beard, 6 plastic knives(honed to a razor sharp edge), specially designed carry-on bag(perfect for hiding explosives with no one being the wiser), and a set of 6 different turbans, so you can really confuse things! Also included is a highly detailed leather-bound instruction manual. Just don't leave home without it!

#672509 Do-It-Yourself Hijacking Kit $299.95

Item #683205 *Jolly-Time Easy-Bake Oven!* Just added to our World War II Collectables. The Jolly-Time Easy Bake Oven comes complete with WWII Style German Oven, 8 different Emaciated-Jew Cookie cut-outs, 5 SS Cookie cut-outs, and for a limited time only, the Swastika Cookie cut-out. Also, as a bonus for ordering from us direct, we will include 24 Emaciated Jew Action Figures! Recreate the Holocaust, and make cookies at the same time!

#683205 Jolly-Time Easy-Bake Oven $49.95
#683205-R Emanciated Jew Action Figure Refill Kits(set of 12) $19.95

Item #693473 *Taliban Barbie!* This limited edition Barbie doll is the perfect gift for a girl of any color. Why? Because the Abayu covers every square inch of this doll! Black Children no longer have any complaints, because they don't know if their Taliban Barbie is white, black, or somewhere in between! A perfect slave to Ken Bin Laden! Order more than one, and build a Harem of your own!

#693473 Taliban Barbie $14.95

Item #693474 *Ken Bin Laden!* The Taliban's' answer to the perfect American Boy! Ken Bin Laden comes complete with assault rifle, suitcase bomb, hand grenades, and training video! A perfect compliment to the Taliban Soldier, and Jihad Joe dolls already on the market!

#693474 Ken Bin Laden $14.95

Item #693475 *Taliban Soldier!* The Taliban Soldier comes complete, and we do mean COMPLETE! From the trainee gear, to the sleeper-agent gear! All 5 phases of the Taliban Training regimen have been skillfully recreated in this masterpiece.

#693475 Taliban Soldier $19.95

Item #693505-A *Plan A Hijacking Play set!* This authentic looking play set comes from the descriptions given by a Taliban POW! Now you too can recreate the planning of the WTC Attack! Complete in every detail! Includes maps, structural schematics, fuel-weight ratios, etc.

#693505-A Plan A Hijacking Play set $29.95

Item #693505-B *Afghanistan Cave Complex Play set!* This play set was carefully crafted from M.I. Plans of the Taliban Cave complexes in Afghanistan. The play set features hidden caves, multiple entrances, supplies for the Taliban, a satellite downlink for capturing intel from CNN, and for a limited time, the smart-missile replica that blew the caves to Hell!

#693505-B Afghanistan Cave Complex Play set $49.95

Item #693505-C *Taliban Training Camp Play set!* Set in the deserts of any middle eastern country, these camps provided us with the entertainment known as The Taliban. Now, you can train your own soldiers in the art of terrorism with this play set. A perfect training ground for your Taliban Soldier, led by Ken Bin Laden!

#693505-C Taliban Training Camp Play set $39.95

Item #693505-D *Pentagon Play set!* Target the Pentagon with this collapsible play set! Comes complete with 100 worker figures, 20 soldier figures, and a scale model plane! Ram the plane into the outer wall of the play set for complete realism! Then run the figures around trying to escape!

#693505-D Pentagon Play set $49.95

Item #693505-E *WTC Play set!* What 9-11-01 collection would be complete without the World Trade Center Play set? This monster play set comes complete with both 110 story towers, all smaller buildings, 50 NYC Firefighter figures, 3 NYC Fire trucks, and a whopping 100 civilian worker figures! Also included are 2 scale model airplanes, and is amazingly collapsible! We took great care in recreating the WTC in all it's glory and detail!

#693505-E WTC Play set $89.95

Item #693628-A *WTC ESCAPE Game!* The game that will redefine board games as we know them! The object of the game is to get from the 30th floor to the lobby before time runs out and the building collapses! The problem? You're competing against others who want to escape, hazards include blocked stairways, and firemen who believe the fire can be contained! It's the ultimate Race Against the Clock!

#693628-A WTC ESCAPE Game $15.95

Item #693628-B *Pentagon ESCAPE Game!* The secondary target of the Taliban provides us with the schematics for a great new game! Escape from the Pentagon after the Airliner has crashed into it. Make your way through the maze of hallways and blocked escape routes, picking up survivors on the way! Whomever escapes with the most survivors wins!

#693628-B Pentagon ESCAPE Game $15.95